AI Revolution

How Artificial Intelligence Is Changing Your World
(And How You Can Profit from It!)

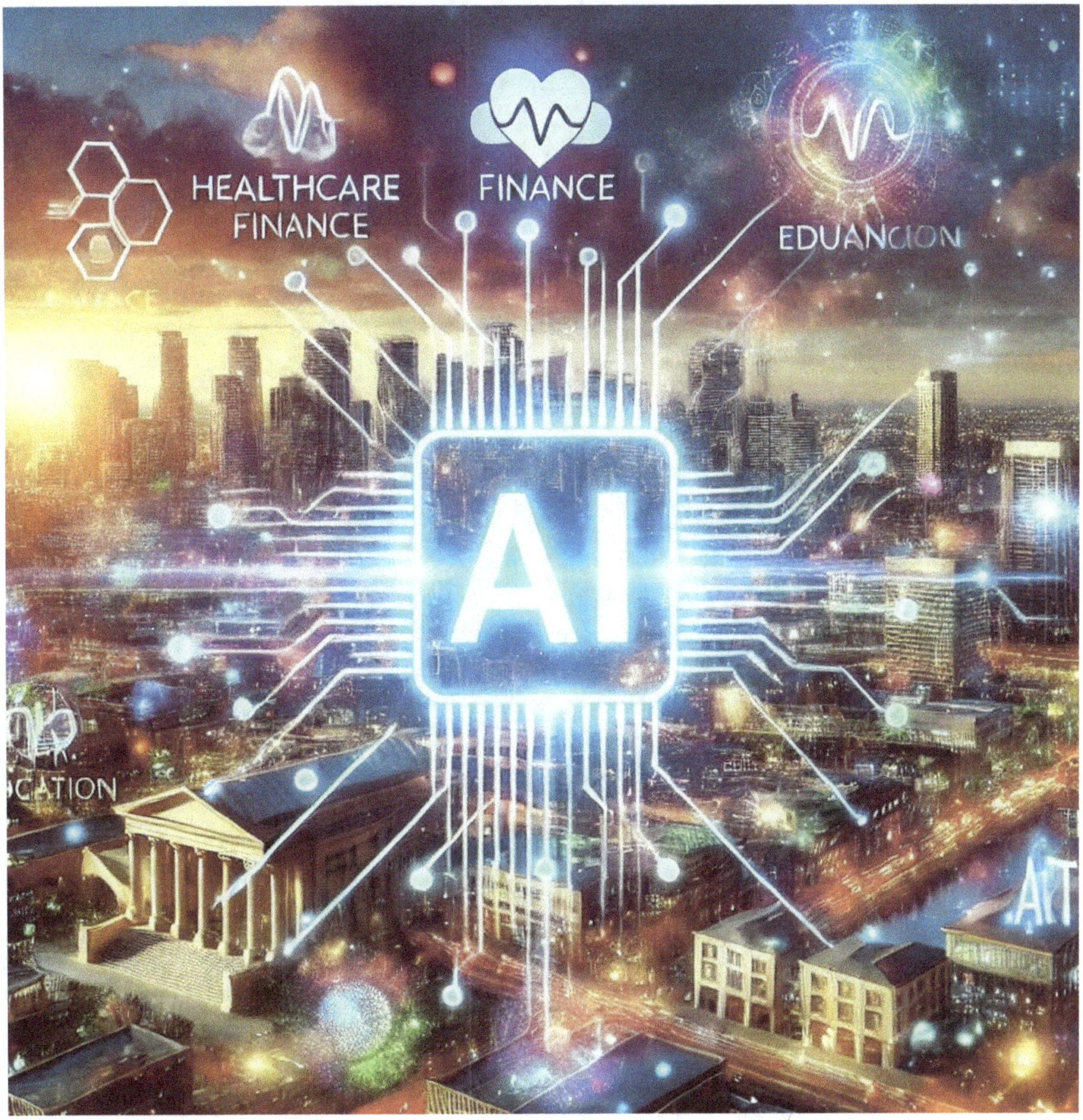

I0478033

By

KMitchell

ii

This book is dedicated to:

Everyone who dares to envision a future shaped by innovation, those who seek knowledge with open minds, and the pioneers who leverage technology to create positive change. May this book inspire you to harness the power of Artificial Intelligence to shape a brighter and more prosperous world for all.

Table of Contents

Introduction

Congratulations on choosing this book! You're about to embark on a journey into the world of artificial intelligence (AI) and its practical uses, bringing powerful tools like ChatGPT and other popular AI programs right to your fingertips. By investing in this guide, you're taking the first step toward understanding and harnessing the transformative potential of AI in your personal and professional life.

In today's fast-paced digital age, many people find themselves overwhelmed by endless tasks, creative roadblocks, or simply the challenge of staying up-to-date with evolving technology. You may have wondered, *How can I boost productivity without feeling burned out?* or *How can I bring more creativity and efficiency to my work?* This book was crafted with you in mind, offering a solution to these common challenges by introducing you to accessible, easy-to-use AI tools that can simplify complex tasks and inspire fresh ideas.

With the practical techniques outlined here, you'll learn not only the basics of how AI works but also how to use it effectively to enhance your productivity, creativity, and decision-making. From generating ideas and brainstorming to automating repetitive tasks, this book will show you how AI can become your personal assistant, creative partner, and productivity booster all in one.

As the author, I've spent years studying the intersection of technology, business, and human behavior. Through research, real-world experience, and hands-on practice with AI tools like ChatGPT, I've developed the insights shared in this book to make AI understandable and usable for beginners. My goal is to demystify AI, giving you the confidence and skills to put it to work for you.

By the end of this guide, you'll be equipped with practical knowledge to improve workflows, enhance creativity, and navigate the ethical considerations surrounding AI. You'll learn how to engineer effective prompts, integrate AI seamlessly into your routines, and maximize its potential without getting overwhelmed.

This book is more than just a read—it's a toolkit for modern living. Dive in, and don't wait to unlock the benefits. The sooner you start exploring the possibilities of AI, the sooner you'll see the impact in your daily life. So, let's get started! Turn the page and discover how AI can transform the way you think, work, and create.

Introduction: Embracing AI in Everyday Life

Artificial intelligence (AI) is no longer a futuristic idea reserved for science fiction or complex technology discussions; it has woven itself into the fabric of our everyday lives, transforming how we work, communicate, and even think. Just a decade ago, few could have predicted that AI would shift from an abstract concept into a practical, accessible tool. Today, AI is everywhere, seamlessly integrating into the apps we use, the websites we visit, and even the devices that help us manage our day-to-day routines. From voice assistants like Siri and Alexa answering simple questions to sophisticated AI tools generating complex ideas, AI is reshaping how we interact with the world.

What makes AI so remarkable isn't just its technological capability but the way it's accessible to nearly everyone. Individuals from all walks of life—whether students, writers, business owners, or hobbyists—can now use AI to solve problems, spark creativity, and save time. Imagine needing a quick summary of a dense article; instead of spending hours dissecting it yourself, an AI tool like ChatGPT can generate an overview in seconds. Or think about creating unique artwork without any design skills. With AI-powered image generators like MidJourney, visual expression is now open to everyone, not just artists. AI has moved from being a complex, niche tool to a versatile resource that people can access with just a few clicks.

The purpose of this book is to explore these capabilities and show you how to make the most of AI in ways that are practical, empowering, and fun. Whether you're here to increase productivity, spark fresh ideas, or simply satisfy your curiosity, you'll find that AI offers endless possibilities. Throughout this guide, you'll learn about various AI tools, with a special focus on ChatGPT, an AI developed by OpenAI that has captivated millions with its ability to generate human-like responses in conversations. But ChatGPT is just one piece of the puzzle; this book will introduce you to other popular AI tools as well, each offering unique advantages for specific needs.

Why AI Matters to Readers

So why should AI matter to you, the reader? In a world that's becoming more digitally driven, AI represents not just a tool but a new way of thinking. Whether you're aiming to streamline your workflow, tackle creative projects, or explore new knowledge, AI can open doors that previously required specialized skills or significant resources. Imagine you're an entrepreneur with limited time and a long to-do list. Instead of handling every task manually, AI tools can automate repetitive tasks, freeing up your time for more strategic work. For example, using Jasper AI, you could automate the creation of social media content, enabling you to maintain an online presence without dedicating hours to writing and scheduling posts. Or if you're a writer experiencing a creative block, ChatGPT can help brainstorm ideas, provide suggestions, and even draft text based on your guidance.

The beauty of AI is that it's not confined to one industry or purpose. Artists, writers, marketers, students, and professionals from countless fields are finding ways to leverage AI to enhance their work. Take, for example, the field of education. With tools like ChatGPT, students can ask questions, clarify doubts, and get study material summaries, making learning more interactive and personalized. On the other hand, a corporate professional may use AI to generate quick summaries of lengthy reports, enabling them to grasp essential points without wading through pages of text. The real value of AI lies in its versatility; it can adapt to your needs, whatever they may be.

But beyond productivity, AI is also a powerful tool for creativity. Suppose you're a visual artist or someone interested in design. In that case, AI-powered art generators like MidJourney can create intricate, beautiful images based on simple text prompts, removing the need for technical art skills while empowering creative expression. Writers, too, can use AI to explore new narratives, experiment with style, or generate fresh ideas that may not have emerged otherwise. By combining computational power with human ingenuity, AI doesn't just make tasks easier—it amplifies what's possible.

Overview of Popular AI Tools

To fully understand the capabilities AI brings to the table, it's helpful to have a basic understanding of the most popular tools in the space, each with its own strengths and specialties. At the forefront is ChatGPT, developed by OpenAI. Known for its conversational abilities, ChatGPT has gained widespread popularity for generating responses that sound remarkably human. Unlike traditional search engines, which provide static answers to queries, ChatGPT can hold conversations, offer advice, create content, and respond dynamically to user input. It's a versatile tool that can assist with a wide range of activities, from drafting emails and brainstorming ideas to even helping with code.

Alongside ChatGPT, Jasper AI stands out as a go-to tool for content creation. Jasper is designed with marketers and content creators in mind, offering capabilities to generate blog posts, marketing copy, social media posts, and other text-based content. Jasper's strength lies in its understanding of tone, style, and structure, making it an invaluable tool for businesses and individuals looking to engage audiences effectively. If you've ever struggled with writer's block or felt overwhelmed by the volume of content you need to create, Jasper AI can be a game-changer.

For those interested in visual creativity, MidJourney is an AI-powered image generator that brings imagination to life. By simply typing a prompt, users can generate artwork, concepts, or designs without any prior artistic training. MidJourney is particularly popular among designers, artists, and hobbyists who want to explore visual creativity without traditional art tools. From generating logos to creating concept art, MidJourney democratizes the art world, allowing anyone to explore visual design.

Google's Bard and Microsoft's Copilot also deserve mention. Bard integrates AI into search, giving users conversational answers instead of the standard list of links, while Copilot enhances productivity applications like Excel and Word with AI assistance. These tools cater to everyday productivity needs, showing how AI can make even routine tasks more efficient and intuitive.

Setting Expectations for the Book

As you delve into this book, you'll embark on a journey of learning, exploration, and skill-building. This isn't a technical manual filled with jargon or a dense, academic exploration of AI; it's a practical guide designed to empower you with hands-on skills and knowledge. Our goal is to make AI accessible and actionable, giving you the tools to integrate AI into your personal and professional life without feeling overwhelmed.

In the chapters ahead, you'll start with the basics—learning how to interact with AI through prompts. Prompt engineering, or the art of crafting effective prompts, is a skill that anyone can develop with practice, and it's the key to getting the most out of tools like ChatGPT. You'll learn how to create prompts that yield useful responses, helping you achieve your goals efficiently. As you progress, we'll explore various applications, from content creation and coding assistance to data analysis and beyond, showing you how to tailor AI for specific needs.

The book will also guide you through the process of integrating AI into your workflows. Rather than using AI in isolation, you'll learn how to incorporate it into your routines to maximize efficiency. Whether it's setting up automations, combining multiple tools for complex tasks, or understanding when and how to rely on AI, the skills you gain will allow you to leverage AI as a seamless part of your daily toolkit. By the time you finish this book, you'll have a strong foundation in AI, enabling you to use it confidently, creatively, and responsibly.

Future Potential and Responsible Use of AI

AI's potential extends far beyond what we currently see. As technology advances, AI is expected to become even more integrated into every facet of our lives, from personalized education systems and healthcare innovations to sustainable business practices and advanced creative tools. Imagine a world where AI-powered assistants can help diagnose illnesses, where artists collaborate with algorithms to create new forms of expression, or where education is tailored to each student's unique needs. The possibilities are limitless, and as you learn about AI, you're stepping into a future filled with opportunity.

However, with great power comes responsibility. AI isn't without its challenges, and ethical considerations are an essential part of the conversation. Issues like data privacy, potential biases in AI responses, and the societal impacts of automation are all factors that responsible AI users must consider. This book will touch on these important topics, equipping you with the knowledge to use AI ethically and thoughtfully. Understanding AI's limitations is just as crucial as understanding its capabilities, and by using it responsibly, we can ensure that AI remains a force for good.

In embracing AI, you're not only enhancing your own abilities but also participating in a broader shift towards a technologically enriched society. This book will help you navigate this new landscape, offering you the tools and insights needed to make informed choices. As you turn the page, remember that AI is a tool to empower, not replace, human potential. So let's embark on this journey together, exploring how AI can enrich our lives while respecting the values that make us human.

CHAPTER 1: Understanding the Foundations of AI

What is AI?

Artificial Intelligence, or AI, has become a buzzword in today's digital age, capturing the imagination of tech enthusiasts, businesses, and everyday users alike. At its core, AI refers to the simulation of human intelligence in machines designed to perform tasks that traditionally require human understanding and decision-making. These tasks can range from simple pattern recognition, like identifying objects in an image, to complex problem-solving processes, such as making decisions based on vast amounts of data. Unlike other technologies that are simply tools, AI possesses a unique capability: it can adapt and learn over time, often improving as it processes more data.

To break down AI's definition further, it's helpful to distinguish it from other technology terms. Many people confuse AI with automation, but the two are quite different. Automation involves programming a machine to carry out a specific task repeatedly without variation, such as sorting items on a conveyor belt. AI, however, brings a layer of decision-making, as it can analyze and adapt based on new information. For instance, an AI-powered program designed for image recognition can be "trained" on thousands of pictures of cats and dogs, allowing it to distinguish between them with high accuracy—even in images it has never seen before.

The roots of AI date back to the mid-20th century, with the idea initially proposed by computer scientists and mathematicians who envisioned machines that could mimic human thought processes. Early AI systems were basic, operating on pre-set rules and lacking the ability to learn autonomously. These initial programs paved the way for modern AI by laying down fundamental concepts, such as algorithms and data processing. As computer power and storage capacity grew, AI research entered new realms, enabling machines to analyze complex data and improve their performance based on experience.

By the late 20th and early 21st centuries, advancements in computing transformed AI from a theoretical concept into a practical tool. AI is now embedded in many aspects of our daily lives, from recommending products based on past purchases to personalizing news feeds. This rapid evolution means that AI is no longer confined to research labs; it's a tool used by businesses, governments, and even individuals to make decisions, automate repetitive tasks, and gain insights from data.

Today, AI encompasses multiple approaches and technologies, which are categorized into various subfields. These include machine learning, deep learning, and natural language processing (NLP), each contributing unique capabilities that allow AI to interact more naturally with humans and the environment. This chapter will dive into these essential areas, providing the foundational knowledge needed to understand and harness AI tools effectively.

Understanding Machine Learning and Deep Learning

Machine learning (ML) and deep learning are two closely related but distinct aspects of AI, forming the backbone of many applications we see today. Machine learning refers to the process where machines or computer systems improve their performance on a task without explicit programming for every possible scenario. Instead of coding every rule, machine learning algorithms analyze data to detect patterns and make predictions or decisions based on those patterns. For instance, a machine learning model can predict house prices by examining data from past sales, considering variables like location, square footage, and amenities.

To better understand how machine learning works, imagine training a model to recognize different types of flowers. Initially, the model doesn't "know" what a flower is, so it processes thousands of labeled images (e.g., roses, daisies, tulips) and learns to recognize distinguishing features for each flower type. As it processes more images, the model gets better at making accurate predictions, even with new flower images it has never seen before. This training process is powered by algorithms, which are mathematical instructions that guide the model in interpreting data, adjusting, and refining its outputs.

Deep learning is a subset of machine learning, but with a notable difference: it uses neural networks that are structured to mimic the human brain. These artificial neural networks consist of layers of interconnected nodes, or "neurons," that process data in multiple stages. Deep learning models can handle far more complex tasks and massive datasets, making them ideal for tasks like image recognition, speech processing, and even autonomous driving.

Let's explore an example to clarify the difference. Imagine using AI to classify images of animals. A basic machine learning model might rely on pre-set features, such as color or shape, to categorize an animal as a dog or a cat. In contrast, a deep learning model would autonomously learn to recognize the features distinguishing each animal, breaking down the image into layers and analyzing each layer for patterns without requiring human-defined rules. This ability to "self-learn" complex patterns allows deep learning to power advanced AI applications like voice-activated assistants, facial recognition systems, and ChatGPT.

AI tools like ChatGPT are made possible by these learning approaches, especially deep learning. By training on vast amounts of text data, ChatGPT learns the structure, patterns, and context of human language, allowing it to generate human-like responses. Machine learning and deep learning, therefore, are the core processes that make AI adaptive and intelligent, allowing it to analyze, predict, and even "understand" information in a way that was previously exclusive to humans.

What is Natural Language Processing (NLP)?

At the heart of conversational AI lies a subfield of AI known as natural language processing, or NLP. NLP is the technology that enables machines to interact with human language, interpreting and generating text in ways that feel natural and meaningful. This capability is essential for AI tools like ChatGPT, which engage in human-like conversations, answer questions, provide summaries, and even carry out basic creative tasks. NLP allows these AI systems to go beyond simple keyword matching, enabling a deeper understanding of context, intent, and sentiment.

NLP involves several complex processes, but two core functions are text recognition and sentiment analysis. Text recognition allows AI to "read" text by identifying words, phrases, and sentence structures. When you type a question into ChatGPT, it uses NLP to parse the text, recognizing not just the words but the context and relationship between them. For instance, if you ask, "Can you suggest a good sci-fi book?" NLP enables ChatGPT to understand that you're seeking a recommendation rather than a definition of science fiction.

Sentiment analysis is another vital component of NLP, allowing AI to interpret the emotional tone of a sentence. This ability is particularly useful in customer service applications, where understanding whether a customer is pleased, frustrated, or neutral can improve response quality. For example, if a customer writes, "I am very disappointed with the product quality," an AI-powered support system using sentiment analysis could recognize the negative sentiment and prioritize the message for quick handling.

Context understanding is another advanced feature of NLP, allowing AI to grasp not only the explicit meaning of words but also the subtleties and nuances that shape human communication. Context understanding allows AI to interpret ambiguous phrases, respond appropriately to follow-up questions, and hold a coherent conversation. This ability is especially important in tools like ChatGPT, where the goal is to create an interaction that feels human and fluid.

NLP is one of the most challenging aspects of AI because human language is inherently complex, filled with idioms, slang, and regional variations. However, advances in NLP have made it possible for AI to engage in sophisticated conversations, generate creative content, and even analyze text for hidden meanings. With NLP, AI is not only functional but also interactive, bringing us closer to a world where machines can genuinely "understand" human language.

The Rise of Conversational AI

Conversational AI refers to the subset of artificial intelligence dedicated to enabling machines to interact with people through text or speech. As the name implies, conversational AI systems are designed to hold conversations, whether by answering questions, guiding users through processes, or simply providing friendly interaction. The rise of conversational AI is one of the most exciting developments in AI because it allows machines to integrate seamlessly into our lives, assisting in ways that feel natural and intuitive.

The evolution of conversational AI is closely tied to advancements in NLP, machine learning, and neural networks. Early chatbots were rule-based, relying on pre-set responses to specific inputs, which limited their ability to engage in complex or nuanced conversations. Today's conversational AI tools, such as ChatGPT, have far surpassed these limitations, thanks to sophisticated algorithms that allow them to generate responses based on vast amounts of data. These AI models don't just follow scripts; they "learn" from examples and adapt to the conversation flow, providing responses that are both relevant and contextually appropriate.

Conversational AI is used across various industries, from customer service to healthcare, education, and entertainment. In customer service, for instance, AI chatbots can handle routine inquiries, such as tracking orders or providing product information, freeing up human agents for more complex issues. In education, conversational AI tools are being used as virtual tutors, helping students with homework, explaining concepts, and offering practice exercises. Personal productivity applications also benefit from conversational AI, with tools like ChatGPT acting as brainstorming partners, language translators, and writing assistants.

The rise of conversational AI signifies a shift in how we interact with technology. No longer confined to isolated functions, AI can now participate in meaningful dialogue, responding to user needs and even learning from previous interactions. This ability to "converse" has made AI tools not only more versatile but also more user-friendly, breaking down barriers and making AI accessible to people from all backgrounds.

Key AI Tools to Know: ChatGPT and Beyond

Among the various conversational AI tools, **ChatGPT** stands out as one of the most widely used and versatile examples. Developed by OpenAI, ChatGPT is based on the GPT-3 and GPT-4 language models, which have been trained on vast amounts of text data from the internet. This extensive training allows ChatGPT to generate human-like responses, making it suitable for a range of tasks, from drafting emails and answering questions to providing creative writing prompts and even assisting with coding.

What makes ChatGPT unique is its ability to generate coherent, contextually relevant responses across diverse topics. Unlike many chatbots that follow predefined scripts, Chat

GPT can engage in open-ended conversations, adapting its responses based on the user's questions and input. However, it does have limitations, such as occasional inaccuracies or a lack of real-time awareness of current events, as its responses are based on patterns rather than direct understanding or reasoning.

Other popular AI tools include Jasper AI, which is designed primarily for content creation and marketing, helping users generate blog posts, social media content, and ad copy. For visual creativity, tools like MidJourney allow users to generate images based on text prompts, opening up new possibilities for artists and designers. Google's Bard and Microsoft's Copilot represent productivity-oriented AI, providing conversational responses in search and office applications, respectively. These tools demonstrate AI's versatility, each catering to unique user needs and enhancing specific workflows.

With this chapter's foundation in place, you now have a broad understanding of AI, from its core concepts to specific tools that are reshaping our approach to work, creativity, and problem-solving. The following chapters will dive deeper into these tools, offering practical guidance on how to integrate them into your life and maximize their potential.

How AI Impacts Daily Life

As we've seen, AI is not just for experts; it's a tool that can enhance our daily lives in countless ways. From automating routine tasks and improving productivity to enabling creative exploration, AI has applications that fit seamlessly into the lives of individuals from all backgrounds. Content creators, for instance, can use ChatGPT to draft ideas, explore new writing styles, or brainstorm plotlines. Customer service professionals benefit from AI chatbots that handle repetitive inquiries, allowing them to focus on more complex customer needs.

In personal productivity, AI tools like scheduling assistants can analyze user habits and optimize daily routines. Visual artists can use image generators to explore new aesthetics, and businesses can use AI to personalize marketing strategies based on customer data. The possibilities are virtually limitless, with AI enhancing nearly every aspect of life in ways that are both practical and inspiring.

In conclusion, AI is not just a futuristic concept; it's a present-day tool that is accessible and valuable for everyone. By understanding these foundational concepts, you're well-equipped to explore the rest of this guide and learn how to leverage AI in ways that are meaningful and beneficial for your unique needs.

CHAPTER 2: Mastering ChatGPT – A Comprehensive Guide to Getting Started and Making the Most of AI

Getting Started with ChatGPT

ChatGPT has quickly become one of the most popular AI tools, empowering millions to harness the power of artificial intelligence in an accessible, conversational format. Developed by OpenAI, ChatGPT leverages a language model that processes and generates human-like responses, allowing users to interact with AI as though they were conversing with a knowledgeable partner. This technology has become invaluable for people across various fields—from writers and marketers seeking inspiration to educators, students, and professionals looking to streamline their work.

The appeal of ChatGPT lies in its versatility and simplicity. Unlike many software tools that require specialized knowledge or training, ChatGPT operates within a straightforward chat interface. Users simply type a question or command, and the AI responds with an answer or a solution. This design allows beginners to access advanced AI functions with ease, without needing an in-depth understanding of programming or machine learning. Let's start by covering how to access ChatGPT, the different versions available, and the platform's essential features to help you feel comfortable with it from the outset.

Accessing ChatGPT

Getting started with ChatGPT begins by visiting OpenAI's website, where the tool is hosted. Users need to create an account, which requires a valid email address and a password. For additional security, OpenAI offers two-factor authentication, a feature worth enabling to keep your account secure. Once registered, users can log in to access the ChatGPT interface.

OpenAI offers both free and paid versions of ChatGPT. The free version provides access to the base model, which is powerful enough for basic tasks but might have limitations on high-demand days. For those looking to maximize ChatGPT's capabilities, OpenAI offers a paid plan called **ChatGPT Plus**. The Plus subscription gives users access to GPT-4, the latest model, which provides faster and more accurate responses than the free GPT-3.5 version.

Interface Overview

Once logged in, you'll find yourself in ChatGPT's user-friendly interface. The platform is structured as a simple chat window where users can type queries or commands in a text box at the bottom of the screen. After hitting 'Enter,' ChatGPT generates a response in real time, displayed in a conversation bubble above the input box. This intuitive design makes it easy for users to engage with the AI and follow conversation threads.

The ChatGPT interface also includes features like **conversation history** (for Pro users), **dark mode**, and **settings adjustments**, where users can modify preferences according to their needs. The history feature allows users to revisit past interactions, making it convenient to pick up previous threads or review answers. OpenAI is constantly updating the platform to improve functionality, and recent updates include options for different "modes" where the AI can behave more creatively or conservatively, depending on the task at hand.

Now that we've covered the basic setup, let's explore how ChatGPT can be used effectively, including understanding its strengths and limitations.

Understanding ChatGPT's Capabilities and Limitations

ChatGPT is an incredibly powerful tool, designed to perform a wide range of tasks by leveraging vast data and advanced algorithms. Its capabilities are rooted in a technology known as **transformer-based language modeling**, which allows the AI to understand and generate language in ways that often feel natural and human-like. This model, trained on diverse datasets, can predict what comes next in a sequence of words, which enables it to hold coherent conversations, answer complex questions, and even generate creative content.

ChatGPT excels in many areas, making it a versatile tool for personal and professional use. Some of its key capabilities include:

- **Generating Written Content**: ChatGPT can help write essays, articles, stories, emails, and even poetry. It's widely used by writers and content creators to overcome writer's block, draft ideas, and fine-tune their language.

- **Answering Questions**: From general knowledge to specific questions, ChatGPT can provide well-structured answers on almost any topic, making it a helpful resource for research and learning.

- **Brainstorming and Idea Generation**: ChatGPT can support creative thinking by suggesting ideas for blog posts, product names, project concepts, and more.

- **Assisting with Coding**: Developers often turn to ChatGPT for help with coding tasks, debugging issues, and understanding programming concepts.

- **Conversational Engagement**: ChatGPT offers an engaging conversational experience, where users can seek advice, learn about new topics, or explore different points of view.

While ChatGPT offers a robust set of capabilities, it is also essential to understand its limitations to avoid misinterpretation or misuse. One of its primary limitations is **accuracy**. ChatGPT is trained on large datasets that contain both factual and fictional information, and it doesn't have real-time access to the internet or external databases. This limitation means that its knowledge base is limited to data available up to its last update (in GPT-4's case, as of 2021 or later versions). Thus, it may sometimes generate responses that sound plausible but are factually incorrect.

Another limitation of ChatGPT is its **lack of real-time awareness**. Unlike search engines, which can provide up-to-the-minute information, ChatGPT's responses are based on pre-existing data. For instance, if you ask about recent news events, ChatGPT may give an outdated answer. Similarly, while ChatGPT can mimic human conversation, it doesn't truly "understand" context in the way a person does, leading it to sometimes misunderstand nuanced questions or provide overly general responses.

Moreover, ChatGPT can occasionally produce **confidently incorrect answers**, a phenomenon known as "AI hallucination." It may assert information with certainty, even if that information is incorrect. This is why users need to fact-check critical answers or use ChatGPT as a supplementary resource rather than a definitive one.

To use ChatGPT effectively despite these limitations, it's advisable to:

1. **Double-check critical information**: Use reliable sources to verify any important or sensitive data provided by ChatGPT.

2. **Be specific in your prompts**: Clear and detailed prompts reduce the chances of ambiguity and improve response quality.

3. **Provide feedback**: Correcting or refining responses can help shape the direction of the conversation, leading to more accurate answers.

Understanding these capabilities and limitations equips users to interact with ChatGPT more effectively, allowing them to make the most out of this powerful tool while remaining mindful of its boundaries.

Practical Applications of ChatGPT

One of the most appealing aspects of ChatGPT is its versatility. Users from various fields can apply ChatGPT's capabilities to different tasks, enhancing productivity, creativity, and learning. Let's explore some of the practical applications of ChatGPT across key areas, providing real-world examples for each.

1. Content Creation

ChatGPT is an invaluable tool for content creators, whether they're writing blog posts, creating social media updates, or drafting scripts. By simply providing a prompt, users can have ChatGPT generate ideas, structure articles, or even suggest catchy headlines. For instance, a blogger might input a prompt like, "Write an introduction about the benefits of a plant-based diet," and ChatGPT can generate a draft that serves as a starting point.

Content creation can also include generating marketing materials, such as email newsletters and ad copy. Small businesses, freelancers, and marketers use ChatGPT to create engaging content that resonates with their audience without spending hours drafting from scratch. By using prompts like "Suggest five email subject lines for a spring sale on eco-friendly products," ChatGPT can provide quick, creative options that streamline the content creation process.

2. Customer Service

Many companies are integrating ChatGPT-like technology into their customer service operations to improve response times and handle frequent inquiries. ChatGPT can be trained to answer common questions, assist with order tracking, and resolve basic issues, freeing up human agents to address more complex matters. For example, an e-commerce company might use an AI-powered chatbot to handle inquiries like, "Where is my order?" or "How do I return a product?" ChatGPT's ability to understand and generate responses quickly makes it ideal for managing high volumes of interactions efficiently.

3. Coding Assistance

Developers frequently use ChatGPT for coding support, as it can generate code snippets, troubleshoot issues, and explain programming concepts in simple terms. For example, a developer working on a Python script might ask, "How do I create a function that sorts a list in ascending order?" ChatGPT can generate a basic code snippet, saving time and helping developers focus on more advanced tasks. While it's not a substitute for a fully integrated development environment (IDE), ChatGPT serves as a useful aid for both beginner and intermediate programmers.

4. Language Translation

While there are specialized tools like Google Translate for language translation, ChatGPT can offer conversational translation services and contextual language help. Users can input phrases and request translations in different languages, or ask ChatGPT to explain language nuances and idioms. For instance, if a user is learning Spanish and wants to understand the phrase "tener éxito," ChatGPT can provide not only the literal translation ("to be successful") but also examples of how the phrase is used in context.

5. Learning and Study Assistance

Students and lifelong learners use ChatGPT as a study aid, taking advantage of its ability to explain concepts, summarize complex texts, and answer subject-specific questions. A student preparing for a history exam, for example, might ask, "Can you summarize the causes of the French Revolution?" ChatGPT can provide a concise, accessible overview, making it easier for the student to understand key points. Similarly, learners can use ChatGPT to practice language skills, explore new topics, and even create flashcards for efficient study.

These applications showcase the adaptability of ChatGPT, enabling users to apply AI to tasks across different domains. By tailoring prompts to their specific needs, users can unlock ChatGPT's full potential, making it a valuable asset in personal, educational, and professional settings.

Prompt Engineering: Getting the Best Results from ChatGPT

One of the essential skills for maximizing the effectiveness of ChatGPT is **prompt engineering**—the art of crafting questions and commands to elicit the best possible responses. Since ChatGPT generates answers based on the input it receives, the clarity and structure of your prompts directly impact the quality of the output. Effective prompt engineering helps users guide ChatGPT toward relevant, accurate, and helpful responses.

Types of Prompts

Understanding different types of prompts can be beneficial for tailoring ChatGPT's responses:

1. **Open-ended Prompts**: These are general questions or requests that allow ChatGPT to explore a topic freely. For example, "Tell me about renewable energy sources" will yield a broad overview, suitable for learning about a new subject or brainstorming.

2. **Specific Prompts**: These prompts are narrowly focused, directing ChatGPT to provide a concise answer. For instance, "List three advantages of solar power over fossil fuels" encourages a clear, direct response, ideal for users seeking targeted information.

3. **Conditional Prompts**: In conditional prompts, users specify conditions that guide ChatGPT's response. An example could be, "Explain the benefits of solar power, but keep it under 100 words." This type of prompt is useful for generating content within specific parameters, such as word count or style.

Best Practices for Prompt Engineering

To optimize your interactions with ChatGPT, consider the following tips:

- **Be Clear and Concise**: Vague questions can lead to vague answers. State your questions or instructions as clearly as possible.

- **Provide Context**: Offering background information helps ChatGPT generate more accurate responses. For instance, rather than asking, "What are some marketing tips?" try "What are some digital marketing tips for a small eco-friendly business?"

- **Use Follow-Up Questions**: If the initial response isn't detailed enough, follow up with additional questions to get the specifics you need.

- **Experiment with Rephrasing**: If ChatGPT's initial response doesn't meet your expectations, try rephrasing your prompt. Slight adjustments can often yield different, more useful results.

Mastering prompt engineering allows users to access ChatGPT's full range of capabilities, providing customized responses tailored to specific needs. This skill is particularly valuable for professionals who rely on AI to generate content, solve problems, or assist in decision-making processes.

Integrating ChatGPT into Daily Workflows

For those looking to maximize productivity and efficiency, integrating ChatGPT into daily workflows can be transformative. Rather than treating ChatGPT as a standalone tool, consider it an integral part of your task management and problem-solving toolkit.

Methods of Integration

Several approaches can help integrate ChatGPT seamlessly:

- **Task Automation**: ChatGPT can automate repetitive tasks, such as drafting emails or generating weekly reports, freeing up time for higher-priority activities.
- **Combining with Other Tools**: Integrate ChatGPT with platforms like Google Workspace or project management software, where it can assist with drafting documents, providing insights, or managing schedules.
- **Creating Custom Workflows**: Establish routines that leverage ChatGPT at specific points in a project, such as brainstorming at the start or editing drafts at the end. Consistent use can enhance productivity by standardizing processes.

Balancing AI use with traditional methods is essential for fostering creativity and critical thinking. While ChatGPT can streamline tasks, users should retain the final say in decision-making to maintain originality and ensure quality.

Ethical Considerations and Responsible AI Use

As AI technology becomes increasingly integrated into everyday life, responsible usage is essential. Using ChatGPT and similar tools raises important questions about data privacy, plagiarism, and potential biases in AI-generated content.

Key Ethical Issues

- **Data Privacy**: Be mindful of sensitive information shared with ChatGPT, as data is sometimes logged for model improvement. Avoid inputting confidential or personal data.

- **Avoiding Plagiarism**: AI-generated content should not be considered entirely original, as it may reflect patterns in the data it was trained on. Always review and edit content to ensure authenticity.

- **AI Bias**: AI models are trained on datasets that may contain inherent biases, affecting responses. Users should critically evaluate AI outputs, especially when making decisions based on generated information.

By using AI responsibly and being aware of these considerations, users can ensure that their interactions with ChatGPT align with ethical standards, fostering a safe and constructive environment for AI-assisted work.

CHAPTER 3: Advanced Techniques and Applications for ChatGPT

This chapter provides an in-depth exploration of intermediate and advanced techniques for using ChatGPT, covering nuanced interaction methods, prompt engineering for complex tasks, applications in data analysis, and automation of routine activities. It concludes with case studies that demonstrate ChatGPT's adaptability across industries and offers guidance for embracing the future of AI responsibly.

Intermediate Techniques for AI Interactions

With a foundational understanding of ChatGPT, users can progress to intermediate techniques to maximize their interactions and achieve more accurate, relevant, and dynamic responses. This chapter delves into nuanced methods that help users refine responses, utilize multi-step queries, and enhance the overall interactivity of their experience with ChatGPT. By exploring these strategies, users can unlock more of ChatGPT's potential, creating a more personalized and efficient experience.

Refining Responses for Better Accuracy

One of the primary challenges users encounter with ChatGPT is obtaining responses that are either too broad or not fully aligned with the original query. To counter this, refining techniques can help produce responses that are precise and contextually relevant. A key method here is **rephrasing and restating questions**. When a response seems vague, users can clarify the question by restating it with added context, guiding the AI toward a more focused answer.

For example, let's say a user asks, "What are the benefits of remote work?" and receives a general response. If they want information specifically related to productivity, they can rephrase to, "What are the productivity benefits of remote work for knowledge workers?" This clarification narrows ChatGPT's focus and encourages it to provide a response tailored to the specific aspect of interest.

Another useful strategy for refining responses is **adding constraints** to the query. Constraints may include word limits, tone requests (e.g., formal or casual), or target audience specifications. For instance, if a user needs a brief summary for an email, they might ask, "Summarize the benefits of remote work in 100 words for an email to employees." By including constraints, users help guide ChatGPT to produce responses that meet their practical needs.

Using Multi-Step Queries

ChatGPT can hold a conversation over multiple steps, a feature that enables users to build on previous responses and explore complex topics in depth. This conversational approach is particularly effective when working on intricate tasks that require layered information or when brainstorming ideas.

Consider a scenario where a user is developing a marketing strategy for a new product. They could begin by asking, "What are some unique selling points for a sustainable home-cleaning product?" ChatGPT might provide a few broad ideas, such as eco-friendly packaging, natural ingredients, and affordability. The user could then refine the query, asking, "Can you suggest target demographics that would be interested in these selling points?" ChatGPT would build upon the previous answer, offering demographic insights like environmentally conscious millennials or families with young children.

By using multi-step queries, users guide ChatGPT through a logical progression, obtaining responses that evolve based on the ongoing context. This layered questioning simulates a consultation process, where each response contributes to a cumulative understanding of the topic.

Enhancing Interactivity through Follow-Up Questions

Follow-up questions allow users to delve deeper into ChatGPT's initial responses, expanding on particular points or exploring alternative viewpoints. A key to this approach is **active engagement**; instead of accepting the initial response as final, users can treat it as a stepping stone for further inquiry.

For example, if ChatGPT provides a list of remote work benefits, the user might follow up with, "Could you explain how each of these benefits impacts employee retention?" or "What are some challenges associated with each of these benefits?" Such follow-up questions encourage ChatGPT to provide more detailed and balanced answers, enhancing the richness of the response and bringing additional insights into view.

Follow-up questioning is also valuable for problem-solving scenarios, where multiple factors or perspectives are involved. By exploring different angles, users can engage ChatGPT in a way that mimics an in-depth discussion, similar to brainstorming with a colleague or mentor.

These intermediate techniques—refining responses, multi-step querying, and active engagement—empower users to shape their interactions with ChatGPT, achieving higher relevance, accuracy, and depth in responses. These techniques create a more dynamic and tailored AI experience, moving beyond basic use to a more deliberate and purposeful application of ChatGPT's capabilities.

Prompt Engineering for Complex Queries

Prompt engineering is an art that elevates the way users interact with ChatGPT, especially when tackling complex queries. Advanced prompt engineering techniques, such as layering prompts, using conditional instructions, and applying specific phrasing methods, can yield more nuanced and comprehensive responses. By mastering these tactics, users can direct ChatGPT to address sophisticated tasks and generate multifaceted content.

Layering Prompts for Detailed Responses

Layered prompts are essential when users require responses that cover multiple aspects of a topic or require detailed information. This technique involves breaking down complex questions into several layers, each targeting a different dimension of the topic.

Consider the task of generating a content plan for a blog focused on sustainable living. Instead of asking ChatGPT, "What should a sustainable living blog cover?" the user could employ a layered approach:

1. **Layer 1**: "What are some broad topics related to sustainable living?"

2. **Layer 2**: "Under each broad topic, can you list specific subtopics or article ideas?"

3. **Layer 3**: "For each subtopic, suggest relevant keywords and phrases for search optimization."

Each layer builds upon the previous responses, creating a structured content plan that incorporates topics, subtopics, and keywords. This approach enables users to obtain well-organized and comprehensive answers to complex queries, making ChatGPT a more effective tool for content planning, research, and strategic analysis.

Conditional Instructions for Customized Outputs

Conditional instructions allow users to specify particular criteria for ChatGPT's responses. By including conditions, users can guide the AI to produce content that aligns with unique requirements, such as tone, format, or perspective.

For example, a business professional preparing a presentation for a diverse audience might use a conditional prompt: "List the pros and cons of remote work. In the pros section, emphasize benefits for employees. In the cons section, emphasize challenges for employers." This prompt directs ChatGPT to focus on the pros and cons from distinct perspectives, ensuring a balanced and relevant response that meets the user's specific needs.

Conditional instructions are also useful when users want ChatGPT to adopt certain viewpoints or provide specialized content. An academic researcher might ask, "Summarize recent studies on climate change's economic impact, but prioritize findings related to the agricultural sector." By framing prompts with conditions, users can obtain content tailored to their exact requirements, enhancing ChatGPT's utility across diverse scenarios.

Specific Phrasing Methods for Clarity and Precision

The phrasing of prompts can significantly impact ChatGPT's responses, especially when dealing with complex or sensitive topics. Specific wording helps clarify the user's intentions, minimizing ambiguity and improving the likelihood of a useful answer.

When a user needs ChatGPT to adopt a particular style or tone, they can explicitly state this in the prompt. For instance, a user writing a formal business report might request, "Provide a professional summary of the recent market trends in renewable energy." Alternatively, for a more casual summary, the user could specify, "Explain recent market trends in renewable energy in simple terms, suitable for a blog post."

For complex problem-solving tasks, users might find it helpful to include phrases like "step-by-step," "list the key factors," or "break down the process." These phrasing techniques ensure clarity, helping ChatGPT provide responses that are organized, logical, and easy to follow.

Mastering these prompt engineering techniques allows users to interact with ChatGPT on a deeper level, customizing responses to suit complex and specific needs. Whether layering prompts for comprehensive information, using conditions for tailored outputs, or applying precise phrasing, these methods help users unlock ChatGPT's full potential.

Using ChatGPT for Data Analysis and Insights

ChatGPT can be an invaluable asset for data analysis, assisting users in identifying trends, summarizing findings, and drawing insights from large sets of information. Although ChatGPT is not designed to handle raw data processing, it can provide meaningful interpretations and assist users in understanding complex data reports. Professionals across various fields—including marketing, education, and healthcare—can benefit from using ChatGPT for data-driven tasks.

Summarizing Data Trends

One of ChatGPT's strengths is summarizing data trends in a clear, digestible format. Users can input findings from research studies, market reports, or surveys, asking ChatGPT to synthesize the key points. For instance, a marketing manager who has access to quarterly sales data might request, "Summarize the main sales trends over the past quarter and suggest potential causes for these trends."

ChatGPT can analyze the provided information, highlighting patterns such as seasonal demand, demographic preferences, or emerging product categories. Although it cannot process data independently, ChatGPT can interpret summaries provided by the user, transforming complex trends into actionable insights.

Generating Insights from Reports

In addition to trend summaries, ChatGPT can help users interpret comprehensive reports by answering targeted questions about the content. A healthcare professional reviewing a medical study, for example, could ask ChatGPT to provide insights on specific aspects of the research. Prompts like "What were the primary findings on patient recovery rates?" or "How does this study compare to previous research on the same topic?" encourage ChatGPT to extract relevant information.

This feature is particularly useful for those needing quick access to insights without delving into every page of a report. By breaking down complex documents into smaller queries, users can obtain a clearer understanding of the report's main points and their implications.

Interpreting Findings Across Fields

ChatGPT's ability to adapt to different contexts makes it a versatile tool for professionals seeking industry-specific insights. Educators analyzing student performance data might ask ChatGPT to identify trends in subjects where students struggle most, while business leaders could request summaries of financial trends affecting their sector.

In each case, ChatGPT can provide context-appropriate explanations, helping users interpret data in light of industry-specific considerations. Although not a replacement for a professional analyst, ChatGPT serves as an effective tool for preliminary analysis and report interpretation, supporting informed decision-making.

These data analysis techniques enhance ChatGPT's role as an AI tool, providing users with interpretive capabilities that bridge the gap between raw data and actionable insights. With clear instructions and targeted queries, ChatGPT can help users summarize, analyze, and apply data trends effectively.

Automating Routine Tasks with AI

Automation is one of AI's greatest strengths, allowing users to streamline repetitive tasks and increase efficiency. ChatGPT can be integrated into daily workflows to assist with routine activities, such as drafting emails, generating reports, and scheduling content. This section explores how to set up ChatGPT for automation, providing examples of common use cases.

Setting Up ChatGPT for Task Automation

To begin automating tasks, users must first identify repetitive activities that ChatGPT can assist with. Tasks like drafting recurring emails, generating weekly reports, and producing content schedules are ideal candidates. By programming ChatGPT to handle these activities, users free up valuable time for higher-priority work.

For instance, a user might create a prompt template for customer service responses. A template like "Respond to a customer inquiry about product returns, emphasizing our 30-day return policy" can be used repeatedly, saving customer service representatives the effort of drafting responses from scratch.

Creating Custom Scripts

Custom scripts allow users to set up ChatGPT for complex, multi-step tasks. A marketing team, for example, might use ChatGPT to generate weekly social media content. By combining prompts for headline generation, post copy, and hashtag suggestions, the team can produce a full week's worth of posts in one session.

Custom Scripts for Efficiency

By creating custom scripts, users can automate even more complex workflows. Let's consider a content creation process for a blog. A writer might use a series of prompts to generate multiple components of a blog post in a single sitting. Here's a sample custom script structure that can streamline the process:

1. **Topic Ideation**: "Suggest five blog post topics about sustainable home cleaning solutions."

2. **Outline Generation**: "Create an outline for the blog post titled '5 Eco-Friendly Home Cleaning Hacks' with three main sections."

3. **Introduction Draft**: "Write an engaging introduction for a blog post titled '5 Eco-Friendly Home Cleaning Hacks.'"

4. **Content Development**: "Expand on each section of the outline with 150–200 words."

5. **Conclusion**: "Conclude the blog post by summarizing the benefits of eco-friendly cleaning."

This multi-step automation saves time and provides structure, allowing the writer to focus on refining and editing rather than drafting from scratch. By creating a reusable script like this, users can generate content efficiently and maintain consistent quality across multiple posts.

Streamlining Customer Responses

For teams in customer service, ChatGPT can be used to create standardized responses for frequently asked questions, making the customer interaction process faster and more consistent. Here's an example of an automated response script for a retail business:

1. **Greeting and Acknowledgment**: "Greet the customer warmly and acknowledge their inquiry about [insert issue here, e.g., 'shipping delay']."

2. **Response Body**: "Explain our policy regarding [insert specific issue] and provide relevant details."

3. **Offer of Assistance**: "Ask if there's anything else the customer needs help with and let them know you're here to assist."

4. **Sign-Off**: "Sign off with a friendly closing, thanking them for their patience."

With this script, ChatGPT can generate quick, consistent responses that align with the company's customer service standards. The representative only needs to fill in specific details, reducing time spent on each individual response.

Scheduling Content with ChatGPT

Social media and content scheduling are other areas where ChatGPT can be utilized. By creating prompts to outline and schedule content for platforms like Twitter, Instagram, or LinkedIn, users can produce a week's or month's worth of posts in one session.

For instance, a content manager could prompt ChatGPT as follows:

1. **Post Creation**: "Write a series of five Instagram posts about sustainable living tips. Each post should have a unique tip, be 100 words or less, and end with a call to action."

2. **Caption Generation**: "Create engaging captions for each post, targeting environmentally-conscious followers."

3. **Hashtag Suggestions**: "Suggest relevant hashtags for each post that can increase engagement."

By setting up ChatGPT to handle the content ideation and initial draft creation, users can focus on refining the posts for brand consistency. This approach not only saves time but ensures that the content is ready well ahead of schedule, improving overall workflow efficiency.

Incorporating ChatGPT into routines like these demonstrates how automation with AI can help users and teams meet deadlines, stay organized, and free up time for strategic tasks that require human creativity and judgment.

Case Studies: Real-World Applications of ChatGPT

To illustrate the versatility of ChatGPT, let's examine several real-world case studies that showcase how professionals across different industries use ChatGPT to optimize workflows, generate ideas, and improve productivity. These examples provide practical insight into the challenges ChatGPT can help overcome and the tangible outcomes it can deliver.

Case Study 1: Marketing and Content Creation

Challenge: A digital marketing agency needed to increase content output without expanding their team. They required high-quality blog posts, social media content, and email marketing materials that could engage clients across various industries.

How Artificial Intelligence Is Changing Your World (And How You Can Profit from It!) by Mitch

Solution: The agency implemented ChatGPT to handle the initial drafts for blog posts and social media captions. Using prompt engineering techniques, they created specific templates that covered different types of content, such as listicles, how-to guides, and promotional posts. For email marketing, ChatGPT generated subject lines, calls to action, and content suggestions.

Outcome: The agency was able to increase their content output by 40% without hiring additional staff. ChatGPT's initial drafts allowed the team to focus on editing and personalization, which streamlined their workflow and enhanced creative collaboration. By utilizing AI for content ideation and drafting, the agency met client demands efficiently and improved their overall output quality.

Case Study 2: Customer Support in E-commerce

Challenge: An online retail company experienced a surge in customer inquiries, especially around product returns, shipping delays, and order tracking. The customer support team struggled to handle the high volume of repetitive questions without compromising response time and quality.

Solution: ChatGPT was integrated into the company's customer support platform to assist in answering FAQs. Using pre-set templates, ChatGPT generated responses for common inquiries, including specific product policies, shipping times, and troubleshooting steps. Human agents handled only the complex or unique issues that required a personalized touch.

Outcome: The customer support team saw a 30% decrease in response times, and customer satisfaction scores improved significantly. By delegating routine inquiries to ChatGPT, the team had more time to address high-priority cases, resulting in faster resolutions and higher-quality service.

Case Study 3: Education and Online Learning

Challenge: A university professor teaching an online course in psychology wanted to provide personalized study aids to students without spending hours creating them manually. The course had large enrollment, and students frequently requested summaries, practice questions, and explanations of complex topics.

Solution: The professor used ChatGPT to generate personalized study guides, summaries, and flashcards. For example, they prompted ChatGPT to create concise explanations of key psychological theories and generated flashcards that covered essential terms and concepts. ChatGPT also helped in drafting multiple-choice practice questions for students to test their understanding.

Outcome: Students reported higher engagement and comprehension, as the personalized study aids enabled them to focus on challenging topics. The professor was able to provide high-quality supplemental materials at scale, enhancing the learning experience without significant additional effort.

Case Study 4: Healthcare Data Interpretation

Challenge: A healthcare analyst was tasked with interpreting patient data trends across several clinics to identify key patterns in treatment outcomes. The datasets included complex information on patient demographics, treatment types, and recovery timelines.

Solution: The analyst used ChatGPT to summarize large datasets and highlight significant patterns in patient outcomes. By breaking the data down into manageable segments and using targeted prompts, ChatGPT provided insights that identified correlations between treatment types and recovery rates.

Outcome: ChatGPT's ability to quickly process and summarize data trends saved the analyst considerable time. The generated insights contributed to strategic recommendations for clinic practices, ultimately improving patient care and operational efficiency.

These case studies highlight ChatGPT's role as a versatile tool that can adapt to various industries and functions. By integrating AI into their workflows, professionals across fields have been able to address specific challenges, streamline processes, and achieve measurable improvements in productivity and service quality.

Navigating the Future of AI in the Workplace

As ChatGPT and similar AI technologies continue to evolve, their influence on the workplace is likely to grow. The future of AI in professional settings holds exciting possibilities, including innovations that enhance productivity, creative collaboration, and data-driven decision-making. However, the rise of AI also brings important ethical considerations and challenges, making it essential for professionals to navigate this landscape thoughtfully and responsibly.

AI-Driven Innovation and Emerging Opportunities

The continued advancement of AI opens doors to new roles and opportunities in nearly every industry. AI-driven innovation has already transformed fields like marketing, healthcare, education, and customer service, and its potential for expansion is vast. For example, in the creative industries, AI can assist designers and artists in generating ideas or refining concepts, while in finance, it aids analysts in predicting market trends and identifying investment opportunities.

Emerging opportunities will likely focus on roles that bridge the gap between human creativity and AI capabilities. Professionals who are skilled in AI tools will have a competitive advantage, as they can leverage technology to enhance their work and meet the evolving demands of their industries. AI fluency is set to become a valuable skill, similar to digital literacy, offering individuals an edge in innovation-driven workplaces.

Ethical Considerations in AI Use

The rise of AI also raises ethical concerns, particularly regarding data privacy, bias, and the potential for over-reliance on automation. Professionals using ChatGPT should be aware of these issues to ensure responsible engagement with AI tools.

1. **Data Privacy**: ChatGPT processes user inputs, which may contain sensitive information. It's important to avoid inputting confidential data that could compromise privacy. Businesses must establish guidelines for data handling, ensuring that sensitive information is not exposed during AI interactions.

2. **Bias in AI Responses**: AI models like ChatGPT are trained on large datasets, some of which may contain biases that can influence the AI's responses. Users should critically evaluate AI-generated content, especially when making decisions based on recommendations or insights from ChatGPT. Being mindful of these potential biases enables users to make informed choices and avoid perpetuating inaccuracies.

3. **Avoiding Over-Reliance on AI**: While AI can greatly enhance productivity, over-reliance on automation may erode critical thinking skills and creativity. Professionals should use ChatGPT as a tool for support and inspiration, but ultimately rely on their expertise for final decision-making. Balancing AI assistance with human judgment is crucial to maintaining originality and integrity in professional settings.

Staying Updated on AI Advancements

AI technology is evolving rapidly, with new updates and tools emerging frequently. Staying informed about these developments can help professionals leverage AI's full potential and integrate new capabilities effectively. Online courses, webinars, and industry publications offer valuable resources for learning about the latest AI trends and best practices.

As ChatGPT continues to develop, OpenAI and other organizations are

likely to release new models with improved features, addressing limitations such as real-time data access and accuracy. Keeping pace with these advancements enables users to make the most of emerging tools, enhancing their ability to adapt and innovate in their respective fields.

Incorporating AI Responsibly

Responsible AI use requires a commitment to ethical practices and an understanding of AI's societal impact. By being proactive in addressing privacy concerns, recognizing biases, and promoting balanced AI use, professionals can contribute to a positive AI-driven future. Adopting AI responsibly not only ensures ethical engagement but also fosters a collaborative environment where AI and human expertise can complement one another effectively.

The future of AI in the workplace presents both opportunities and challenges. With the right strategies, professionals can navigate this landscape, utilizing AI to drive meaningful change while maintaining a commitment to ethical and responsible practices.

CHAPTER 4: Advanced Applications of ChatGPT and AI in Professional Fields

1. Introduction to Advanced Applications of ChatGPT

Artificial Intelligence (AI) has swiftly transformed from a futuristic concept into a practical, game-changing tool across numerous professional fields. At the forefront of this AI revolution is ChatGPT, a language model developed by OpenAI, designed initially to answer questions and facilitate conversational tasks. However, ChatGPT has evolved far beyond these general functions. Today, professionals in sectors as varied as marketing, customer service, healthcare, and legal research leverage ChatGPT to optimize workflows, improve decision-making, and enhance productivity.

One of ChatGPT's defining strengths is its adaptability. Unlike traditional software, which is designed with fixed functionalities, ChatGPT can be customized to meet unique industry demands. For example, a digital marketer might use ChatGPT to draft engaging blog posts or create social media content, while a healthcare provider could rely on ChatGPT to simplify complex medical information for patients. This versatility allows ChatGPT to become a valuable asset across professional fields, enabling professionals to tailor its capabilities to specific tasks, audiences, and objectives.

A key advantage of ChatGPT in professional settings is its ability to streamline repetitive tasks, allowing experts to focus on complex, high-level responsibilities. For instance, customer service representatives often face repetitive inquiries—status updates, returns policies, and basic product information. ChatGPT can automate responses to these common questions, reducing wait times and freeing agents to handle more intricate or sensitive cases. This application is equally beneficial in content creation, where ChatGPT assists writers by generating initial drafts, providing topic ideas, and even overcoming creative blocks. By taking on these supporting roles, ChatGPT helps professionals save time and boost productivity.

Beyond efficiency, ChatGPT supports decision-making by synthesizing information and offering strategic suggestions based on data patterns and contextual cues. For example, a market researcher may use ChatGPT to interpret consumer feedback or highlight trends from survey data, which could inform marketing strategies or product development. Similarly, in healthcare, ChatGPT can provide concise summaries of recent studies, enabling medical professionals to stay informed about advancements without spending hours on literature reviews.

Despite its numerous benefits, ChatGPT has limitations that professionals must recognize. Since it generates responses based on its training data, ChatGPT can occasionally provide inaccurate or outdated information. In fields where accuracy is essential, users must treat ChatGPT's output as supplementary, cross-referencing reliable sources as necessary. Moreover, ethical considerations—such as data privacy and potential biases embedded in AI responses—are critical for responsible AI use in professional environments.

In this chapter, we'll explore the specific ways ChatGPT is reshaping various industries. We'll look at how it supports workflows, enhances decision-making, and addresses unique industry challenges in fields such as digital marketing, healthcare, legal research, customer service, and beyond. We'll also discuss potential drawbacks and ethical considerations, offering a balanced view of ChatGPT's professional applications.

2. ChatGPT in Content Creation and Digital Marketing

The digital marketing landscape has undergone significant change over recent years, with content creation standing at the core of modern marketing strategies. In this field, ChatGPT has become an invaluable tool for generating engaging, high-quality content that resonates with target audiences. Marketers use ChatGPT to assist with a range of tasks, from blog posts and social media content to SEO-optimized articles and email marketing campaigns. By supporting each stage of the content creation process, ChatGPT enables marketers to produce consistent, relevant, and audience-focused material efficiently.

In content creation, the objective is to capture the audience's attention and deliver messages that align with brand values and objectives. ChatGPT's ability to generate diverse types of content makes it especially useful in digital marketing. For instance, it can produce blog articles on specific topics, craft captions for social media posts, and create product descriptions that align with a company's tone of voice. Through strategic prompts, marketers can instruct ChatGPT to generate content that emphasizes key messages, incorporates specific keywords, and adheres to established brand guidelines.

One of the most valuable uses of ChatGPT in content marketing is **idea generation**. Creative blocks are common, especially when content must be produced regularly. ChatGPT can assist by providing fresh content ideas tailored to specific demographics, seasonal trends, or industry developments. For instance, a marketer working on a campaign for an eco-friendly brand might ask ChatGPT to suggest five blog post ideas related to sustainable living. ChatGPT might respond with topics such as "10 Everyday

Swaps for Eco-Friendly Living" or "How to Reduce Plastic Waste in Your Home." This capability makes ChatGPT a go-to tool for brainstorming and expanding content themes.

ChatGPT's content generation capabilities rely on advanced natural language processing (NLP) models that analyze prompt context and generate responses accordingly. In digital marketing, SEO is a critical aspect of content creation, and ChatGPT can generate text with strategically embedded keywords that boost search engine rankings. For example, a marketer might request an article draft on "the benefits of organic skincare products," instructing ChatGPT to include keywords like "natural beauty" and "chemical-free skincare." The AI generates an initial draft structured for readability and SEO, which the marketer can then refine and publish.

For social media, ChatGPT can create posts tailored to the platform's style and audience engagement expectations. Since social media audiences expect short, engaging posts, ChatGPT can be prompted to generate captions that resonate quickly. For example, a fashion brand launching a new collection might request Instagram captions with an upbeat and trendy tone, resulting in content that engages followers and supports brand image.

Real-World Examples

One example of ChatGPT's application in digital marketing is its use in email marketing campaigns. Crafting effective subject lines is crucial in driving open rates, and ChatGPT can generate multiple options for testing. For instance, a brand might prompt, "Create five subject lines for our eco-friendly spring sale," allowing ChatGPT to produce engaging, attention-grabbing subject lines. Additionally, ChatGPT can help draft email content, including introductions, product descriptions, and calls to action, supporting marketers in creating emails that drive engagement and sales.

In blog content creation, a wellness company might use ChatGPT to draft articles on health and wellness topics aligned with current trends. By inputting specific instructions for tone, length, and focus areas, the marketer can produce drafts that are easy to personalize and publish, reducing the time spent on initial writing.

**Implications and Connections **

The application of ChatGPT in digital marketing showcases how AI can enhance both the efficiency and quality of content creation. By assisting in everything from ideation to drafting, ChatGPT empowers marketers to maintain consistent output, adapt to audience preferences, and strengthen brand messaging across various channels. However, while

ChatGPT provides valuable support, it's essential to treat its outputs as drafts, refining them to ensure authenticity and alignment with brand standards.

3. Using ChatGPT in Data Analytics and Market Research

In data analytics and market research, large volumes of data are analyzed to derive insights that drive business strategies and understand consumer behavior. ChatGPT, while not a substitute for specialized data analytics tools, plays a valuable supportive role by summarizing information, identifying key trends, and generating preliminary insights. For data analysts and market researchers, ChatGPT transforms complex data into manageable narratives, aiding in faster and more efficient decision-making.

Data analytics involves processing and interpreting data to identify trends, patterns, and insights that inform business decisions. ChatGPT's ability to analyze textual information makes it an asset for analysts who need quick summaries or who want to understand overarching trends in consumer feedback. Though it doesn't handle raw numerical data directly, ChatGPT can interpret structured datasets in narrative form and generate insights based on descriptions or summaries, giving professionals a springboard for deeper analysis.

For example, if a business receives regular customer feedback, ChatGPT can summarize common themes in the feedback, such as frequent complaints or positive remarks about specific product features. This capability is especially valuable for companies that rely on textual data, such as customer reviews or survey responses, to gauge customer satisfaction or preferences.

ChatGPT's role in data analytics is anchored in its language processing abilities. By parsing written summaries, it can identify recurring themes and trends without the need for in-depth computational analysis. For instance, a data analyst might input a summarized report on customer satisfaction, asking ChatGPT to highlight the most frequent complaints or suggestions. ChatGPT's response would identify the main points and contextualize them within the broader customer experience narrative.

In market research, ChatGPT can assist with hypothesis generation. For instance, a researcher might ask ChatGPT, "What are possible reasons behind the recent increase in interest in eco-friendly products?" ChatGPT can provide a list of hypotheses based on social trends, environmental awareness, and consumer behavior, which researchers can then explore more thoroughly.

**Real-World Examples

A real-world example involves a retail company analyzing customer feedback from online reviews. ChatGPT can take these reviews and generate a report summarizing the top customer concerns, preferences, or product praises. Another application might involve competitor analysis, where ChatGPT is prompted to compare market strategies across companies based on available data, offering insights into areas where the company could improve or innovate.

**Implications and Connections **

ChatGPT's utility in data analytics highlights its potential as an assistive tool that complements traditional analytics methods. By enabling faster access to insights and providing preliminary interpretations, ChatGPT supports more agile decision-making and allows analysts to prioritize areas for in-depth investigation. However, as with any AI-driven tool, ChatGPT's interpretations should be validated by data experts for accuracy.

Understood! I'll continue with Chapter 4, following the specified structure and word count tracking guidelines internally, without outputting the counts. Here's the next section:

---

4. AI in Customer Relationship Management (CRM) and Support

Customer Relationship Management (CRM) is critical for building and maintaining strong connections between a business and its customers. ChatGPT has become an invaluable tool in CRM, enhancing response times, personalizing interactions, and boosting overall customer satisfaction. By automating repetitive tasks and providing personalized responses, ChatGPT allows customer service teams to focus on more complex issues requiring empathy and problem-solving skills.

CRM is about managing customer interactions effectively and delivering personalized service that meets or exceeds expectations. ChatGPT's natural language capabilities make it especially useful for CRM systems, as it can respond to common queries, generate tailored responses based on previous customer interactions, and assist in understanding customer sentiment. For example, a business might use ChatGPT to handle inquiries about order tracking, returns policies, or product availability, creating a seamless customer experience.

In addition, ChatGPT offers the ability to provide **multilingual support**, which is crucial for companies with a global customer base. By responding in multiple languages, ChatGPT helps businesses cater to diverse audiences without requiring extensive translation resources. This capability enhances accessibility and customer satisfaction, allowing companies to communicate effectively with customers around the world.

Integrating ChatGPT into CRM systems is often achieved through application programming interfaces (APIs) that allow ChatGPT to interact with existing CRM platforms. For instance, a business can set up ChatGPT to respond to certain types of inquiries automatically, streamlining the handling of repetitive questions. By processing natural language inputs, ChatGPT can recognize customer names, purchase history, and preferences, creating a personalized interaction that builds stronger customer relationships.

ChatGPT can also be configured to handle different types of inquiries with varying levels of complexity. For example, basic questions like "What is your return policy?" can be answered automatically, while more detailed or emotionally sensitive questions can be flagged for human agents. This approach creates a hybrid model where ChatGPT handles routine interactions, while human representatives address complex customer needs, optimizing resource allocation.

An example of ChatGPT's application in CRM can be seen in retail, where it assists with common customer inquiries such as order tracking. A retailer might set up ChatGPT to automatically answer questions related to delivery times, return processes, or stock availability. Similarly, in the telecommunications industry, ChatGPT could guide customers through troubleshooting steps for technical issues, offering preliminary solutions before connecting them with a support agent if necessary.

Another real-world application is seen in banking, where financial institutions use ChatGPT to assist with frequently asked questions about account details, transactions, and loan inquiries. By automating these responses, banks provide faster service to customers, improving satisfaction and reducing waiting times for more specialized help.

**Implications and Connections **

ChatGPT's use in CRM showcases how AI can support businesses in delivering faster and more personalized service. While it cannot replace the human touch in certain cases, especially those involving sensitive issues, ChatGPT allows companies to handle routine inquiries efficiently, leading to a more satisfying customer experience. As ChatGPT technology advances, it may offer even deeper integration within CRM systems, further enhancing customer interaction quality and efficiency.

---

5. Legal and Compliance Applications of ChatGPT

The fields of law and compliance are known for their demand for precision, extensive documentation, and strict adherence to regulations. While ChatGPT cannot replace the expertise of legal professionals, it can assist with tasks like document review, preliminary research, and compliance checks. This support allows legal teams to allocate more time to high-level analysis, strategic planning, and client-focused work.

In legal and compliance applications, ChatGPT is valuable for its ability to parse large amounts of text and generate summaries, highlight important clauses in contracts, or assist in drafting initial versions of documents. By taking on these repetitive tasks, ChatGPT allows lawyers and compliance officers to focus on more intricate and strategic matters. For instance, legal professionals might use ChatGPT to review lengthy contracts, extracting key clauses and presenting them in an easily digestible format.

ChatGPT can also help ensure regulatory compliance by interpreting relevant policies and providing summaries of regulatory requirements. This application is particularly useful for multinational companies navigating various legal landscapes. By streamlining information related to local laws and regulations, ChatGPT aids compliance teams in creating and maintaining policies that adhere to regional standards.

In a legal context, ChatGPT operates as a document analysis tool, capable of processing complex legal texts and highlighting important sections. Legal teams might input a contract and prompt ChatGPT to identify specific clauses related to termination, confidentiality, or liability. Though it does not conduct formal legal analysis, ChatGPT can provide a quick overview, allowing legal professionals to focus on details that require nuanced interpretation.

For compliance, ChatGPT can interpret regulatory guidelines and summarize key points relevant to the organization. For example, a compliance officer could ask ChatGPT to provide an overview of data privacy requirements under the General Data Protection Regulation (GDPR), giving the company a foundation for building compliant processes.

A common application of ChatGPT in the legal field is its use in drafting routine documents such as non-disclosure agreements (NDAs). Legal teams can prompt ChatGPT with parameters for the NDA, allowing the AI to generate a draft that is then reviewed and refined by a lawyer. In compliance, a global organization might use ChatGPT to update its team on international regulatory changes, streamlining the process of adapting policies across different regions.

In another example, law firms might use ChatGPT for preliminary case research, where the AI reviews summaries of case precedents, helping lawyers identify potentially relevant cases more efficiently.

The application of ChatGPT in legal and compliance tasks demonstrates its potential to improve efficiency in complex, text-heavy industries. Although legal oversight remains crucial to ensure accuracy and adherence to ethical standards, ChatGPT's assistance with document review and compliance summaries allows professionals to manage workloads more effectively, focusing on areas that require human expertise.

---

6. Healthcare Applications of AI and ChatGPT

The healthcare industry is increasingly adopting AI to enhance patient care, medical research, and administrative efficiency. ChatGPT, while not a substitute for clinical expertise, offers valuable support in areas such as patient education, preliminary diagnostics, and medical literature review. By making complex information accessible and streamlining communication, ChatGPT helps healthcare professionals focus on delivering high-quality care.

ChatGPT's applications in healthcare revolve around its ability to communicate medical information in a clear and accessible way. For patients, medical terminology can often be confusing or overwhelming, and ChatGPT can help by providing explanations that are easy to understand. For example, a doctor might use ChatGPT to generate an explanation of a diagnosis, ensuring patients understand their condition and treatment options.

Additionally, ChatGPT can assist healthcare providers during initial assessments by gathering symptom information. While not a replacement for diagnosis, this function can offer preliminary guidance on potential conditions, helping providers prioritize cases more effectively, especially in high-demand settings.

ChatGPT's language processing capabilities allow it to generate responses based on healthcare-related prompts, though with limitations. Healthcare professionals can use ChatGPT to input patient symptoms or queries, receiving a summary of possible conditions or treatment options. For patient confidentiality, ChatGPT must be integrated within secure, compliant systems to protect sensitive data.

In medical research, ChatGPT can summarize articles and synthesize findings across studies. For example, a researcher might prompt ChatGPT with a query to summarize recent advancements in a specific medical field, allowing for a quick overview before delving into detailed research articles.

In patient education, a healthcare provider could use ChatGPT to explain chronic conditions like diabetes in simple terms, improving patient understanding and adherence to treatment plans. Hospitals might also employ ChatGPT for triage support in emergency rooms, where it can assist in prioritizing patients based on symptom descriptions, expediting care in time-sensitive situations.

Additionally, medical researchers may use ChatGPT to process large volumes of studies and extract relevant insights, saving time and allowing them to focus on critical analysis.

The application of ChatGPT in healthcare highlights its role as a support tool that improves communication, aids in initial assessments, and accelerates research. With responsible use, ChatGPT can assist healthcare providers in delivering more informed, patient-centered care. However, given the ethical considerations around patient data, ChatGPT's implementation in healthcare requires stringent data privacy and security measures.

---

7. Future Potential of ChatGPT in Professional Fields

Looking ahead, the potential of ChatGPT in professional settings is vast. With continual advancements, ChatGPT may transition from a supportive tool to an active participant in creative and strategic processes, further influencing industries like finance, law, healthcare, and beyond.

Future developments in AI could see ChatGPT gaining deeper contextual understanding and enhanced real-time data integration capabilities. This progress would enable it to provide more relevant insights and contribute to strategic planning. For instance, in marketing, ChatGPT could analyze social media trends and consumer feedback to guide dynamic campaigns in real-time.

In fields like finance, ChatGPT might integrate with data-driven AI models to assist analysts by interpreting live market trends, providing a more immediate impact on decision-making.

Advancements in natural language understanding (NLU) could allow ChatGPT to interpret nuanced language, recognizing subtle cues like sarcasm or implied sentiment. Future models might also connect with real-time data, making ChatGPT more useful for professionals in industries that rely on up-to-date information, such as healthcare and customer service.

Imagine a scenario where healthcare providers input general symptoms, and ChatGPT accesses live health databases to provide updates on current diseases, enhancing preliminary assessments.

Consider a legal firm using an advanced ChatGPT for case research. The AI could access and summarize recent cases, providing attorneys with timely updates on relevant legal precedents. Alternatively, a logistics company might use ChatGPT integrated with inventory data to streamline operations and offer real-time updates.

The future of ChatGPT in professional fields highlights AI's potential to integrate more deeply into decision-making and strategic roles. As ChatGPT becomes more advanced, it may set new standards for productivity, innovation, and efficiency in various industries, pushing the boundaries of what AI can achieve.

CHAPTER 5: Maximizing the Potential of AI in Business and Innovation

1. Introduction to AI in Business and Innovation

Artificial Intelligence (AI) has revolutionized the business landscape, becoming a cornerstone of innovation and growth across industries. As companies strive to remain competitive, AI offers tools and techniques to enhance operational efficiency, drive smarter decision-making, and foster creativity in product development. Beyond streamlining processes, AI is enabling entirely new business models, transforming how companies understand and meet customer needs, manage data, and even redefine workplace roles. Understanding how AI integrates into business is essential for professionals and organizations aiming to harness its full potential.

AI refers to machines or systems that mimic human cognitive functions like learning, reasoning, and problem-solving. This capability, supported by machine learning (ML) and deep learning (DL), enables AI to process vast amounts of data, identify patterns, and make predictions. The goal is not to replace human judgment but to augment it, providing tools to better analyze complex information, anticipate trends, and streamline tasks.

In business, AI applications range from predictive analytics and customer personalization to operational automation and real-time decision-making. For example, a retail company might use AI to predict buying trends based on historical data, while a healthcare provider could employ AI to analyze patient records and suggest treatments. Moreover, AI can revolutionize customer experiences by understanding preferences and personalizing interactions, creating loyalty and enhancing satisfaction.

The integration of AI also leads to innovation by providing new capabilities in product development and market strategy. Businesses that adopt AI are better equipped to innovate, as AI-driven insights often reveal unique customer needs or product features that may otherwise be overlooked. For example, companies like Tesla use AI to optimize vehicle performance, personalize driving experiences, and manage real-time data from their fleet, positioning them as leaders in autonomous driving.

The economic impact of AI is vast, with estimates suggesting that AI could contribute up to $15.7 trillion to the global economy by 2030. By automating processes, AI reduces operational costs while increasing output and quality. In sectors like finance, AI-driven models assess risks and investment opportunities, while in manufacturing, AI-powered robots ensure precision and efficiency on production lines. The adoption of AI represents a paradigm shift that changes not only how businesses operate but also how they envision growth and innovation.

This chapter delves into the various applications of AI across business functions, exploring how it enhances analytics, drives automation, personalizes customer interactions, fosters product development, and optimizes marketing. We'll explore real-world examples and consider both the transformative potential and the challenges associated with integrating AI into business.

---

2. AI-Driven Data Analytics and Decision Making

In a data-driven world, businesses are constantly generating and collecting massive amounts of data. AI has become an essential tool for interpreting this data efficiently and accurately, allowing companies to make informed decisions that drive growth and adapt to market changes. From customer behavior and operational efficiency to financial forecasting and risk assessment, AI's role in data analytics is extensive.

Data analytics involves examining datasets to uncover trends, patterns, and insights that can guide business strategies. Traditional data analysis relies heavily on statistical methods and human interpretation, which can be time-consuming and prone to error, especially with large datasets. AI-driven analytics, however, employs machine learning algorithms that automate the analysis process, offering faster, more precise insights.

Machine learning algorithms process data by identifying patterns and drawing conclusions, improving over time as they learn from new data. For example, in predictive analytics, AI can anticipate customer behaviors based on past purchases, browsing habits, and demographic information. In business, this means companies can proactively address customer needs, optimize inventory, or tailor marketing strategies.

With AI, decision-making becomes more agile and data-backed. Machine learning models provide probabilistic predictions, identifying which strategies are most likely to succeed based on previous outcomes. These insights empower business leaders to make decisions with confidence, knowing that their choices are supported by comprehensive data analysis.

AI-driven data analytics often relies on supervised and unsupervised learning. In supervised learning, algorithms are trained on labeled datasets where the desired outcome is known. For instance, in fraud detection, an AI model is trained on transactions labeled as fraudulent or legitimate, enabling it to flag suspicious activities. In contrast, unsupervised learning works with unlabeled data to identify hidden patterns, making it suitable for tasks like customer segmentation or anomaly detection.

Natural language processing (NLP) also plays a role, especially in analyzing text data from social media, customer reviews, or news articles. NLP allows AI to interpret qualitative data, transforming unstructured text into actionable insights. For instance, sentiment analysis uses NLP to assess customer emotions toward a product, helping companies adjust their branding or customer service approach accordingly.

Deep learning models, particularly neural networks, are used for more complex analyses, such as image recognition or speech processing. In finance, these models assess risk by analyzing factors like historical market data and economic indicators, offering insights that are difficult to obtain through traditional analysis alone.

One prominent example of AI-driven data analytics is Netflix's recommendation system. By analyzing viewing patterns, Netflix's algorithms predict what shows or movies a user might enjoy, driving engagement and customer satisfaction. Similarly, Amazon uses AI for dynamic pricing, adjusting product prices based on factors like demand, competitor pricing, and seasonal trends, maximizing sales while staying competitive.

In healthcare, IBM's Watson Health uses AI to analyze medical records, research papers, and clinical data, assisting doctors in diagnosing diseases and identifying potential treatments. By processing vast amounts of data quickly and accurately, Watson Health helps healthcare professionals make informed decisions, potentially improving patient outcomes.

In retail, AI-powered data analytics aids inventory management. For example, Walmart uses predictive analytics to anticipate stock requirements based on factors like customer demand and seasonal patterns, optimizing supply chains and reducing waste.

The implications of AI-driven data analytics are profound, as businesses can leverage data not only to improve operations but also to foster innovation. With faster and more accurate insights, companies can respond quickly to changes, seize opportunities, and mitigate risks. As AI analytics continues to evolve, businesses will likely rely even more heavily on data for decision-making, making AI an indispensable tool for long-term success.

---

3. Automation and Process Optimization

AI-driven automation is transforming how businesses operate by automating repetitive tasks, optimizing workflows, and reducing costs. Automation enables companies to allocate resources more efficiently, focusing human effort on creative and strategic work. From robotic process automation (RPA) to machine learning-driven workflow optimization, AI is revolutionizing traditional business processes.

Automation involves using technology to complete tasks with minimal human intervention. AI enhances automation by adding a layer of intelligence, allowing systems to make decisions, learn from data, and adapt to new inputs. Robotic Process Automation (RPA), for example, automates rule-based tasks like data entry, invoicing, and report generation. Machine learning algorithms can extend these capabilities, enabling systems to handle more complex workflows that require contextual understanding and adaptation.

In process optimization, AI analyzes existing workflows to identify inefficiencies and suggest improvements. For instance, an AI system in a manufacturing plant might analyze production data to pinpoint delays, equipment malfunctions, or resource bottlenecks. By addressing these issues, companies can increase productivity, reduce costs, and improve product quality.

RPA is the most common type of automation in business, involving software robots or "bots" that follow pre-defined rules. RPA excels in processes with structured data and minimal variation, making it ideal for tasks like payroll, order processing, and account reconciliation. These bots can perform tasks around the clock, increasing productivity and accuracy.

Machine learning algorithms take automation a step further by handling tasks that involve unstructured data or require decision-making. For example, an AI system in customer service might analyze past interactions to predict customer needs, enabling proactive responses. Machine learning models used in automation are trained on historical data, learning to identify patterns that inform their actions.

Workflow optimization tools use AI to map processes and highlight areas for improvement. These tools may employ predictive analytics to anticipate potential issues or bottlenecks, helping businesses to streamline operations. In logistics, for instance, AI-powered optimization tools can recommend more efficient routes for deliveries, reducing fuel costs and delivery times.

In the banking sector, AI-driven automation handles tasks like loan processing and credit scoring. By automating these processes, banks improve processing times and reduce human error. Additionally, AI-based fraud detection systems can monitor transactions in real time, flagging suspicious activity and reducing financial losses.

In manufacturing, companies like Siemens use AI for predictive maintenance. By monitoring equipment performance, AI identifies signs of wear or malfunction before issues arise, reducing downtime and maintenance costs. This proactive approach to equipment management enhances production efficiency and extends the lifespan of machinery.

In the insurance industry, companies use RPA to process claims, automating tasks like data entry and validation. This speeds up the claims process, improves accuracy, and enhances customer satisfaction by reducing waiting times.

The implications of automation and process optimization are significant, as businesses achieve greater efficiency, lower costs, and reduced error rates. AI-powered automation enables companies to scale operations, handle increased workloads, and improve overall performance. As automation technology advances, it will likely play a central role in shaping the future of work, changing workforce dynamics and creating new opportunities for innovation.

---

4. AI in Customer Experience and Personalization

In today's competitive marketplace, customer experience is a critical differentiator for businesses. AI is transforming how companies interact with customers by enabling highly personalized experiences, predictive insights, and real-time responsiveness. Through applications such as recommendation engines, chatbots, and sentiment analysis, AI is helping companies meet customer needs in a way that is timely, relevant, and efficient.

Customer experience (CX) focuses on understanding, anticipating, and meeting customer expectations across every interaction point. AI enhances CX by analyzing data at a granular level to deliver tailored experiences. AI tools allow companies to understand customer preferences and behaviors, facilitating interactions that are more relevant and engaging. For example, a retailer can use AI to recommend products based on browsing history, previous purchases, and seasonal trends, creating a shopping experience that feels personalized to each customer.

Personalization is a key aspect of modern marketing strategies, as it helps build stronger customer relationships and increases loyalty. AI-driven personalization enables businesses to go beyond traditional segmentation, instead focusing on unique individual preferences. Recommendation engines, such as those used by Netflix and Spotify, analyze user data to suggest movies, shows, or songs that align with the individual's tastes, driving higher engagement and satisfaction.

AI-driven personalization relies on machine learning algorithms and data analysis techniques that capture and interpret vast amounts of user data. These algorithms are trained on patterns from historical data, learning to make predictions about a user's preferences based on behavior, demographics, and feedback. Common models include collaborative filtering, which makes recommendations based on the preferences of similar users, and content-based filtering, which suggests items based on specific features.

Natural Language Processing (NLP) is another core technology in AI-driven customer experience. NLP enables AI to understand and respond to text or voice inputs, allowing for conversational interactions with customers through chatbots and virtual assistants. For example, an NLP-powered chatbot on an e-commerce website can assist users by answering questions about products, helping them find items, or guiding them through the checkout process.

Sentiment analysis, a subset of NLP, interprets customer emotions based on text analysis. By analyzing feedback from sources like social media or customer reviews, sentiment analysis provides companies with insights into how customers feel about their products or services. This allows companies to proactively address dissatisfaction or leverage positive feedback to strengthen their brand.

One prominent example is Amazon's recommendation engine, which uses collaborative filtering and machine learning to suggest products based on user browsing and purchase history. This personalized approach has been key to Amazon's success, as customers are more likely to make additional purchases when presented with relevant product recommendations.

In the entertainment industry, Netflix's recommendation system analyzes viewing patterns to suggest movies and TV shows, creating a unique viewing experience for each user. This keeps viewers engaged on the platform, reducing churn and increasing customer satisfaction.

In the airline industry, Delta Airlines uses AI-driven personalization to provide tailored flight experiences. From the booking process to in-flight entertainment, Delta's AI tools help offer relevant options to customers, enhancing the travel experience.

AI's role in customer experience demonstrates its potential to create meaningful connections between businesses and their customers. By enabling personalized interactions, AI not only improves customer satisfaction but also increases retention and loyalty. However, as companies collect and analyze customer data, they must address privacy concerns and ensure ethical data usage to maintain customer trust.

---

5. Product Innovation and Development Using AI

AI is rapidly transforming product innovation and development by providing powerful tools for ideation, prototyping, and improvement. From AI-driven design software to generative design and simulations, companies across industries are using AI to accelerate the product development process, create new functionalities, and enhance product quality. By integrating AI into development workflows, businesses can shorten time-to-market and increase their competitiveness.

Product development involves conceptualizing, designing, and testing products that meet consumer needs and stand out in the market. AI contributes to this process by assisting with the generation of ideas, testing different design concepts, and optimizing products for functionality and cost. Generative design, for instance, uses AI algorithms to explore thousands of design possibilities, allowing engineers to choose the most efficient or innovative solutions.

AI can also play a role in simulating product performance under different conditions, which helps identify potential issues early in the development cycle. By running virtual simulations, companies can refine designs before committing to physical prototypes, saving time and resources. This is particularly valuable in industries like automotive and aerospace, where testing prototypes can be costly and complex.

Generative design is a technique that uses algorithms to generate a wide range of possible product designs based on specified constraints, such as material, weight, or strength. Engineers input the parameters, and the AI evaluates numerous design options, often resulting in innovative shapes and configurations that may not have been considered through traditional design methods.

In manufacturing, AI-driven simulation software predicts how a product will perform, providing insights into potential issues related to stress, heat, or other factors. By analyzing these factors virtually, companies can optimize materials and design to enhance durability and efficiency.

Another application is predictive maintenance, where AI monitors the performance of existing products in the field and identifies signs of wear or failure. By anticipating maintenance needs, companies can improve product reliability, reduce downtime, and increase customer satisfaction.

In the automotive industry, companies like BMW use generative design to develop lightweight, fuel-efficient car components. AI allows BMW to test various designs and select the ones that optimize fuel economy while maintaining strength, enhancing vehicle performance and environmental impact.

In consumer electronics, Apple leverages AI in product development for features like camera enhancements and facial recognition. Machine learning algorithms analyze massive datasets to improve image quality, low-light performance, and speed, resulting in an enhanced user experience.

Healthcare companies use AI to simulate new medical devices, ensuring they meet regulatory standards and perform reliably under different conditions. For example, Medtronic uses AI to simulate device functionality, allowing for safer and more effective product releases.

AI in product development and innovation accelerates the pace of new technologies, enabling companies to stay competitive and bring higher-quality products to market. The implications extend to sustainability as well, as AI can help create products that use fewer resources or perform more efficiently. However, balancing AI-driven innovation with human creativity is essential, as designers must interpret AI outputs to ensure products resonate with customers.

---

6. AI's Role in Marketing and Sales Strategy

AI is revolutionizing marketing and sales by providing data-driven insights, enabling targeted advertising, and optimizing customer segmentation. From CRM systems and sales forecasting to real-time marketing analytics, AI allows companies to better understand customer behavior, tailor their messaging, and maximize return on investment (ROI) in marketing campaigns. Through predictive analytics and automation, AI empowers sales and marketing teams to work more effectively and efficiently.

In marketing, understanding the customer journey is crucial for crafting effective strategies. AI enhances this process by analyzing customer data to reveal insights into preferences, purchase behaviors, and engagement patterns. Machine learning algorithms can segment customers into specific groups, allowing marketers to tailor messages to different demographics or buying stages. This level of personalization increases engagement and improves conversion rates.

AI-driven customer relationship management (CRM) systems take personalization further by tracking individual interactions, purchase history, and preferences. CRM systems powered by AI analyze past interactions and predict future needs, enabling sales teams to approach customers with relevant offers. Sales forecasting also benefits from AI, as machine learning models predict sales volumes based on historical data and market trends, giving businesses a competitive edge.

Machine learning and data analytics are at the core of AI-powered marketing. Algorithms analyze customer data, including purchase history, website behavior, and social media interactions, to create accurate customer profiles. For targeted advertising, AI uses real-time bidding and predictive algorithms to place ads where they are most likely to reach the intended audience.

In CRM, AI-based tools use NLP to analyze communication patterns, allowing sales teams to identify customer sentiment and adjust their approach. Predictive analytics models analyze sales data to forecast trends, helping businesses allocate resources to maximize revenue.

53

Sentiment analysis, often used in social media monitoring, allows companies to gauge public opinion and respond proactively to feedback. For instance, an AI tool might identify a surge in negative comments about a product, prompting the marketing team to address concerns before they escalate.

Coca-Cola uses AI to analyze customer data from various touchpoints, tailoring marketing campaigns to individual preferences. The company's AI tools track interactions, analyze sentiment, and suggest product recommendations, resulting in highly personalized marketing efforts.

In retail, Sephora uses AI in its CRM system to track customer purchases and preferences, offering tailored product recommendations both online and in-store. This personalized approach enhances customer loyalty and drives repeat purchases.

Salesforce, a leader in CRM technology, employs AI for sales forecasting and customer segmentation. Its AI-powered features help businesses predict sales performance, identify high-value customers, and improve engagement by delivering relevant messaging.

AI's influence in marketing and sales demonstrates its potential to refine customer strategies and maximize revenue. By automating and optimizing customer insights, AI helps businesses build stronger relationships and adapt to customer needs in real time. However, companies must navigate ethical considerations, particularly around data privacy, to maintain trust and transparency with customers.

---

7. Ethics, Challenges, and the Future of AI in Business

AI's rapid integration into business brings ethical considerations, including data privacy, job displacement, and potential biases in AI decision-making. As businesses increasingly rely on AI, understanding and addressing these challenges is crucial for sustainable and responsible AI adoption.

The ethical implications of AI extend across data privacy, transparency, and accountability. AI systems often require extensive data to operate effectively,

raising concerns about how this data is collected, stored, and used. Companies must balance innovation with customer rights, ensuring that personal data is used responsibly and securely.

AI also has the potential to disrupt the job market by automating tasks traditionally handled by humans. While AI creates new opportunities, it may also lead to job displacement, requiring businesses to manage the social impact of automation carefully.

AI ethics involves frameworks for data handling, model transparency, and bias mitigation. Bias in AI can arise from training data that reflects historical inequalities, leading to unfair outcomes. To address this, developers use techniques like algorithmic fairness, which adjusts models to ensure equitable treatment.

In data privacy, companies comply with regulations like GDPR by implementing data anonymization and secure storage practices. AI-driven models also undergo regular audits to assess accuracy, transparency, and ethical compliance.

Microsoft has implemented ethical AI guidelines to ensure responsible use of AI, focusing on transparency, fairness, and accountability. IBM has developed tools to detect and mitigate bias in AI, setting an industry example for responsible AI practices.

In financial services, JPMorgan Chase uses AI for fraud detection but prioritizes transparency by explaining AI-driven decisions to customers. This approach builds trust and aligns with regulatory requirements.

AI's future in business depends on responsible adoption, balancing innovation with ethical considerations. As AI continues to evolve, businesses will need to adopt frameworks that promote fairness, transparency, and accountability. The potential for AI to transform industries is immense, but its success hinges on an ethical approach that benefits society as a whole.

CHAPTER 6: AI Across Global Industries - Transformation, Challenges, and Future Directions

1. Introduction to AI's Role Across Industries

Artificial Intelligence (AI) is reshaping the landscape of nearly every industry, from healthcare and finance to retail, manufacturing, and entertainment. The capabilities of AI extend far beyond traditional automation, impacting processes, decision-making, and innovation in profound ways. As businesses and organizations recognize the transformative potential of AI, it's becoming clear that we are only beginning to scratch the surface of its capabilities.

At its core, AI involves the development of systems and algorithms that can process information, learn from data, and make informed decisions or predictions. Unlike conventional software, which relies on predefined instructions, AI uses data to adapt and improve over time. This adaptability makes AI suitable for a wide range of applications, from identifying patterns in large datasets to simulating complex scenarios and optimizing operations. In business, these capabilities translate into increased efficiency, reduced costs, and enhanced accuracy in various processes.

One of the most impactful aspects of AI is its ability to analyze vast amounts of data in real time. In fields like finance, healthcare, and logistics, this capacity for rapid data processing allows organizations to respond more swiftly to changes, predict outcomes with greater precision, and make data-driven decisions. For example, financial institutions use AI for real-time fraud detection, identifying suspicious activities as they occur and protecting assets. Similarly, in healthcare, AI algorithms can analyze patient data to detect potential health risks or suggest personalized treatment options, paving the way for more proactive and preventive care.

The integration of AI across industries also facilitates innovation. By automating routine tasks and providing insights that would be difficult to obtain through manual analysis, AI frees up human resources to focus on creative and strategic work. This shift is particularly evident in fields like product development and marketing, where AI-driven insights enable teams to understand customer preferences, forecast trends, and develop products or campaigns that resonate with their target audience.

However, while AI offers significant benefits, its implementation comes with unique challenges. Data privacy and security are paramount, as AI systems rely on large amounts of personal or sensitive information. Maintaining the security of this data and adhering to privacy regulations, such as the GDPR in Europe, is crucial to fostering trust and ensuring ethical AI use. Furthermore, there are concerns about bias in AI algorithms, which can perpetuate or even amplify existing inequalities if not carefully managed. This issue is particularly pressing in industries like finance and law, where biased AI decisions could have far-reaching consequences.

In addition to ethical concerns, the rapid advancement of AI raises questions about workforce dynamics. As AI takes on more roles traditionally handled by humans, there is a need to consider the potential for job displacement and the skills that will be necessary for the future workforce. While AI creates new roles and opportunities, it also requires that employees upskill and adapt to a changing environment. Many industries are investing in training programs to prepare their workforce for a future where AI is a central component of daily operations.

Despite these challenges, the benefits of AI across industries are undeniable. Businesses that adopt AI strategically are better positioned to compete in a rapidly evolving market, as they can respond to customer demands more effectively, optimize their operations, and innovate at an accelerated pace. Industries that have embraced AI are already seeing tangible results, from improved customer satisfaction and reduced operational costs to enhanced decision-making capabilities.

In this chapter, we will explore the role of AI in several major industries, examining specific applications, case studies, and the implications of AI integration. Each section will delve into how AI is reshaping processes, addressing challenges, and creating new opportunities for growth. From the precision of AI in healthcare to the personalization it brings to retail, we will uncover the diverse ways AI is impacting the world around us. Additionally, we'll consider the ethical and practical challenges that come with AI adoption and discuss strategies for balancing innovation with responsibility.

---

2. AI in Healthcare

The healthcare industry has undergone a significant transformation with the integration of Artificial Intelligence, where AI's capabilities offer potential breakthroughs in diagnostics, personalized medicine, patient care, and administrative efficiency. From predictive analytics and robotic surgery to telemedicine and drug discovery, AI is enabling healthcare providers to make faster, more accurate decisions, ultimately leading to better patient outcomes.

In healthcare, AI's primary function is to assist in data processing and analysis, improving the speed and accuracy of medical decisions. Healthcare generates enormous amounts of data—patient records, medical imaging, lab results, and more—which can be overwhelming for healthcare professionals to process. AI algorithms, particularly those based on machine learning (ML) and deep learning (DL), can analyze these datasets, identify patterns, and generate insights that guide diagnostics and treatment. In diagnostic imaging, for example, AI algorithms trained on thousands of images can detect anomalies such as tumors or fractures, often with a precision that matches or exceeds human experts.

Personalized medicine is another critical area where AI has made substantial strides. Traditional treatments often rely on a one-size-fits-all approach, which may not account for individual differences in genetics, lifestyle, or environmental factors. AI-driven models can analyze a patient's genetic data, medical history, and even lifestyle factors to predict how they might respond to specific treatments. This information allows healthcare providers to tailor treatments to each patient, maximizing efficacy and reducing the risk of adverse effects.

In addition to clinical applications, AI enhances operational efficiency in healthcare by automating administrative tasks. From scheduling appointments and managing billing to handling electronic health records (EHRs), AI-driven tools streamline processes that typically require significant manual effort. Natural Language Processing (NLP) is often used in these tasks to interpret and categorize medical notes, ensuring that patient information is organized accurately and accessible to healthcare providers when needed.

AI's role in healthcare is supported by various machine learning models, each suited to different types of tasks. For diagnostic imaging, convolutional neural networks (CNNs) are commonly used due to their ability to process and interpret visual data. CNNs are trained on labeled datasets of medical images, learning to recognize specific features associated with diseases or abnormalities. This ability to identify patterns within images is invaluable for radiologists, as it enhances the accuracy and efficiency of diagnoses.

In predictive analytics, algorithms like decision trees, support vector machines (SVMs), and deep learning models analyze patient data to forecast health outcomes. For instance, AI can assess the risk of developing chronic diseases like diabetes or heart disease by evaluating factors such as age, medical history, lifestyle, and genetic markers. Predictive models are also employed in hospital settings to predict patient admissions and optimize resource allocation, helping hospitals prepare for high-demand periods and manage staffing more effectively.

Robotic Process Automation (RPA) is commonly used for administrative tasks, where software robots perform repetitive actions such as updating patient records or processing insurance claims. RPA allows healthcare providers to focus on patient care rather than administrative paperwork, improving both productivity and job satisfaction.

In the field of diagnostics, IBM Watson Health has pioneered AI applications for oncology. IBM Watson for Oncology is trained on vast amounts of medical literature, case studies, and patient data, allowing it to provide oncologists with insights and treatment recommendations based on the latest research. In practice, IBM Watson assists oncologists in identifying personalized treatment options for cancer patients, drawing from a wide array of information that would be difficult for a human to process manually.

Another example is the Mayo Clinic's use of AI for predictive analytics in patient care. The clinic developed an algorithm to predict septic shock, a life-threatening condition, based on patient data from electronic health records. By identifying early signs of sepsis, the algorithm allows healthcare providers to intervene more quickly, improving survival rates and reducing the severity of complications.

In robotic surgery, the Da Vinci Surgical System, powered by AI, enables surgeons to perform minimally invasive procedures with greater precision and control. The system uses real-time data to adjust its movements, allowing for enhanced accuracy in complex surgeries such as heart or prostate surgeries. This technology reduces recovery times, minimizes surgical risks, and ultimately improves patient outcomes.

The implications of AI in healthcare are profound, as it holds the potential to revolutionize patient care, making healthcare more accessible, efficient, and personalized. However, the use of AI in healthcare also raises critical ethical and regulatory questions. Data privacy is paramount, as AI algorithms rely on sensitive patient data for training and decision-making. Healthcare providers must ensure compliance with regulations such as the Health Insurance Portability and Accountability Act (HIPAA) in the U.S. and the General Data Protection Regulation (GDPR) in Europe to protect patient information. Additionally, the possibility of biases in AI algorithms—stemming from the data used to train them—poses a challenge, particularly in diagnostic and predictive models where accuracy is crucial.

As AI continues to evolve, its integration into healthcare will likely deepen, enabling more advanced diagnostics, streamlined operations, and truly personalized medicine.

However, careful management and oversight are essential to ensure that these technologies enhance, rather than compromise, patient care.

---

3. AI in Finance and Banking

The financial services industry has embraced Artificial Intelligence for its potential to enhance security, improve customer service, and optimize operations. In finance, AI applications range from real-time fraud detection and algorithmic trading to customer support and personalized banking solutions. As financial institutions navigate increasingly complex data and growing consumer expectations, AI provides tools that enable efficiency, accuracy, and adaptability in a highly regulated environment.

AI in finance primarily supports two broad functions: improving operational efficiency and enhancing decision-making. AI's capabilities to process massive datasets quickly and accurately allow it to identify trends, assess risks, and respond to changes in the financial landscape. Fraud detection is one of the most critical applications, as it relies on AI to monitor transactions in real-time, flagging suspicious activities and preventing financial losses. By recognizing patterns associated with fraudulent behavior, AI systems can alert analysts to potential risks before they escalate.

Algorithmic trading is another area where AI has a substantial impact. In this application, AI algorithms execute trades based on market data, price trends, and pre-defined strategies. Unlike human traders, AI algorithms can process information and make decisions in milliseconds, optimizing the timing of trades to maximize returns or minimize losses. This high-speed, data-driven approach allows financial institutions to stay competitive in fast-moving markets and manage portfolios more effectively.

In customer service, AI-driven chatbots and virtual assistants provide personalized support, handling common inquiries and guiding customers through transactions. Natural Language Processing (NLP) enables these chatbots to understand and respond to customer questions in a conversational manner, improving the customer experience and reducing wait times. Additionally, AI in banking enhances customer personalization, analyzing spending patterns and financial behavior to offer tailored financial products, such as loans or credit cards, that align with individual customer needs.

In fraud detection, AI uses machine learning models such as decision trees, random forests, and neural networks to identify anomalous transaction patterns. These models are trained on vast amounts of historical transaction data, learning to recognize indicators of fraud, such as unusual spending locations or large withdrawals. When a transaction deviates from established patterns, the AI model flags it for further investigation, enabling financial institutions to address potential threats quickly.

Algorithmic trading utilizes deep learning models that can interpret large datasets and predict price movements based on historical data and real-time market information. Recurrent Neural Networks (RNNs), for instance, are particularly effective for time-series analysis, as they can account for past data points when making future predictions. Reinforcement learning, another approach, allows algorithms to learn optimal trading strategies by simulating different scenarios and refining their actions based on performance.

In customer service, AI chatbots are powered by NLP algorithms that can process natural language inputs and generate contextually appropriate responses. These chatbots analyze the syntax and semantics of customer queries, enabling them to provide relevant answers or direct the customer to additional resources. Machine learning also allows chatbots to improve over time, adapting to new types of inquiries based on previous interactions.

One of the most notable examples of AI in finance is JPMorgan Chase's COiN (Contract Intelligence) platform. COiN uses machine learning to analyze legal documents and extract relevant data points, reducing the time required for contract review from hours to seconds. By automating the review process, COiN enables JPMorgan to save valuable time and resources while improving accuracy.

In fraud detection, PayPal leverages AI to monitor transactions for signs of fraudulent activity. PayPal's machine learning algorithms analyze each transaction's context, including factors such as location, frequency, and amount, to identify unusual patterns. When an anomaly is detected, the system alerts PayPal's fraud prevention team, allowing them to take action swiftly and protect users.

In customer service, Bank of America's virtual assistant, Erica, is a prominent example of AI-driven support. Erica assists customers with tasks such as transferring money, checking account balances, and providing budgeting advice. Powered by NLP, Erica can handle a range of customer inquiries, reducing the need for human intervention and providing users with a more convenient banking experience.

AI's application in finance demonstrates its potential to enhance security, improve customer satisfaction, and streamline operations. However, the financial industry must navigate regulatory requirements and ethical considerations when implementing AI solutions. Transparency is essential, as consumers need to understand how their data is used and how

AI algorithms make decisions that affect their financial well-being. Additionally, AI algorithms must be free of biases that could lead to unfair practices, such as discriminatory lending.

As AI technology advances, it will likely become even more integrated into finance, influencing areas such as risk assessment, portfolio management, and regulatory compliance. The challenge lies in leveraging AI to maximize benefits while maintaining transparency, fairness, and security.

---

4. AI in Manufacturing and Supply Chain

The manufacturing and supply chain sectors are among the biggest beneficiaries of AI advancements, with applications ranging from production optimization and quality control to predictive maintenance and logistics management. By enabling real-time decision-making and enhancing operational efficiency, AI is transforming traditional manufacturing and supply chains into agile, data-driven ecosystems.

AI's role in manufacturing is primarily focused on improving production processes and maintaining high-quality standards. One key application is predictive maintenance, where AI analyzes data from sensors on machinery to predict when equipment might fail. By forecasting potential breakdowns, companies can perform maintenance proactively, reducing costly downtimes and avoiding unexpected disruptions in production.

AI also supports quality control by analyzing visual data from product inspections. In traditional quality control, human inspectors review products for defects, a process that can be time-consuming and prone to errors. With AI-powered computer vision, manufacturing companies can automate quality checks, identifying even minute defects with a high degree of accuracy. This technology ensures that only products meeting quality standards proceed to distribution, minimizing waste and improving customer satisfaction.

In the supply chain, AI optimizes logistics and inventory management by forecasting demand and adjusting stock levels accordingly. Machine learning models analyze historical sales data, seasonal trends, and external factors like market conditions to predict demand. This information allows companies to maintain the ideal inventory levels, ensuring that products are available when needed without overstocking or understocking. Furthermore, AI-powered route optimization algorithms in logistics improve delivery efficiency by finding the most efficient paths for shipments, reducing fuel costs and delivery times.

In predictive maintenance, machine learning algorithms such as time-series analysis and anomaly detection models analyze data collected from sensors on manufacturing equipment. These sensors measure variables like temperature, vibration, and pressure, with AI algorithms processing this data to identify unusual patterns that indicate potential issues. The system alerts maintenance teams before failures occur, enabling timely intervention. This approach is particularly effective with neural networks, which can handle large datasets and detect subtle changes that might go unnoticed by human operators.

Computer vision, an AI technology used in quality control, involves convolutional neural networks (CNNs) that can interpret visual data. By training CNNs on images of defective and non-defective products, AI models learn to recognize irregularities during the production process. This capability is especially valuable in industries like electronics and automotive manufacturing, where precision is crucial. Computer vision systems can operate continuously, performing quality checks at speeds that far exceed human capabilities.

For demand forecasting in the supply chain, machine learning models like regression analysis and gradient boosting algorithms are commonly used. These models predict future demand by analyzing factors like sales history, economic indicators, and consumer behavior. In logistics, route optimization leverages AI algorithms such as genetic algorithms and reinforcement learning to determine the most efficient delivery routes. These algorithms adjust in real time based on traffic patterns, weather conditions, and other variables, ensuring timely and cost-effective deliveries.

Siemens is a leader in using AI for predictive maintenance. The company's AI-driven systems monitor machinery in its factories, detecting signs of wear and recommending maintenance before breakdowns occur. This approach has resulted in significant cost savings and improved uptime, allowing Siemens to operate with greater efficiency.

In quality control, Bosch has integrated AI-powered computer vision into its manufacturing process to inspect automotive components. The AI system identifies defects that could compromise safety, ensuring that only high-quality parts are used in vehicle assembly. This technology not only improves safety but also reduces the costs associated with recalls and repairs.

In the supply chain, Walmart uses AI to manage inventory and optimize logistics. Walmart's machine learning models predict product demand with high accuracy, enabling the company to stock items in anticipation of customer needs. Additionally, AI optimizes delivery routes, ensuring that goods reach stores and distribution centers efficiently.

AI's integration into manufacturing and supply chains brings numerous benefits, from reduced costs and improved product quality to enhanced customer satisfaction. However, AI's role in these sectors also has implications for the workforce, as automation may reduce the demand for certain manual tasks. While AI creates new job opportunities in fields like data science and AI operations, it requires companies to invest in retraining their workforce to keep pace with technological advancements.

The potential for AI-driven sustainability in manufacturing and logistics is also significant. By optimizing resource use and reducing waste, AI contributes to environmentally friendly practices, aligning with corporate sustainability goals. However, careful implementation is essential to balance efficiency gains with ethical considerations, particularly around job displacement and environmental impact.

---

5. AI in Education and E-Learning

The field of education is undergoing a transformation with the incorporation of Artificial Intelligence, which enhances learning experiences, streamlines administrative processes, and provides personalized instruction. AI-driven tools in education are helping teachers and students alike, fostering an environment where learning can be more adaptive, interactive, and accessible. By integrating AI, educational institutions are finding new ways to support diverse learning needs and improve outcomes.

AI in education focuses on delivering personalized learning experiences that cater to individual student needs, strengths, and learning styles. Unlike traditional teaching methods, which often follow a one-size-fits-all model, AI-driven e-learning platforms adapt content based on student performance, providing tailored resources and assessments. For example, an AI-powered learning platform might adjust the difficulty of math problems based on a student's past performance, offering additional help or advanced materials as needed. This individualized approach helps ensure that students are neither overwhelmed nor bored, maximizing engagement and comprehension.

AI also supports teachers by automating time-consuming tasks such as grading and attendance tracking. For instance, AI algorithms can grade multiple-choice questions quickly and even assess short-answer responses using Natural Language Processing (NLP). This automation allows teachers to focus more on interactive and high-value activities, such as planning lessons or providing personalized feedback to students.

In addition to personalized instruction, AI in education provides opportunities for language learning through tools that offer real-time translation and pronunciation guides. NLP-powered language applications allow students to practice speaking and receive immediate feedback on pronunciation, vocabulary, and grammar. These applications create an immersive language learning experience, making it easier for students to learn new languages in both structured and informal settings.

The technical foundation of AI in education lies in machine learning and NLP. Adaptive learning platforms, which personalize the educational experience, use supervised learning models to analyze student data and adjust content accordingly. These models consider variables like the time taken to answer questions, accuracy, and engagement levels, generating insights that guide the learning process.

In automated grading, NLP algorithms assess written responses for content accuracy, grammar, and syntax. For example, essay-scoring AI models are trained on large datasets of graded essays, learning to evaluate key aspects such as coherence, structure, and argumentation. These NLP tools make grading quicker and more consistent, though human oversight is often necessary to ensure fair assessments, especially for subjective responses.

AI-based language learning applications use speech recognition and NLP to evaluate pronunciation. Speech recognition algorithms analyze sound waves to detect phonetic patterns, providing users with feedback on pronunciation accuracy. Through reinforcement learning, these applications improve their accuracy over time, enabling more effective language practice.

Duolingo, a popular language-learning platform, leverages AI to personalize lessons for users. Its algorithms track user performance, adjusting difficulty levels and providing targeted exercises to strengthen weak areas. The app's NLP-powered chatbot also allows users to practice conversational skills, giving immediate feedback to help learners improve.

Carnegie Learning, an AI-driven education company, offers personalized math tutoring programs for K-12 students. Using machine learning, the platform identifies gaps in student knowledge and provides tailored exercises to build their skills. Teachers receive insights into student progress, enabling them to intervene when necessary and support each student's unique learning journey.

In higher education, Arizona State University has implemented AI to support student engagement and retention. The university's AI platform analyzes student data to identify those who may be at risk of falling behind, allowing advisors to provide timely support. This proactive approach improves retention rates and helps students stay on track academically.

AI in education offers significant benefits by making learning more accessible, personalized, and engaging. However, its integration also raises ethical considerations, particularly around data privacy. AI-driven platforms collect and analyze large amounts of student data, making it essential to protect this information and comply with privacy regulations such as FERPA (Family Educational Rights and Privacy Act) in the United States. Additionally, while AI can assist teachers, it should be viewed as a complementary tool rather than a replacement for the human touch, which remains critical in fostering a supportive learning environment.

The potential for AI to democratize education is profound, as it allows students from diverse backgrounds and locations to access high-quality, personalized learning experiences. As AI in education continues to evolve, it will likely play a central role in supporting lifelong learning and preparing students for a technology-driven world.

---

6. AI in Retail and E-Commerce

The retail and e-commerce industries have experienced significant transformation with the integration of Artificial Intelligence, which enhances customer experience, optimizes inventory management, and personalizes marketing strategies. AI enables businesses to deliver relevant recommendations, streamline operations, and meet consumer expectations in a highly competitive market. From personalized shopping experiences to efficient supply chain management, AI has become an indispensable tool in retail and e-commerce.

AI in retail is primarily focused on understanding and meeting customer needs more effectively. One of the most common applications is in personalized recommendations, where AI algorithms analyze browsing and purchasing behavior to suggest products likely to interest the customer. For example, an e-commerce platform might recommend items based on a user's previous purchases, preferences, and search history, creating a more engaging shopping experience. Personalized recommendations have proven to increase sales and customer satisfaction, as they make it easier for shoppers to discover relevant products.

In addition to personalization, AI supports efficient inventory management by predicting demand and adjusting stock levels accordingly. Machine learning models analyze historical sales data, seasonal trends, and external factors like market conditions to forecast demand accurately. This capability ensures that products are available when needed, reducing overstocking or understocking issues and enhancing supply chain efficiency.

AI also assists retailers in pricing optimization, allowing businesses to adjust prices dynamically based on demand, competition, and other market factors. Through dynamic pricing, retailers can maximize profits by raising prices during high demand periods and offering discounts when demand is low. This adaptability is particularly valuable in e-commerce, where pricing can influence consumer behavior significantly.

In personalized recommendations, AI leverages machine learning algorithms like collaborative filtering and content-based filtering. Collaborative filtering makes recommendations based on the preferences of users with similar tastes, while content-based filtering suggests products with attributes that match those previously purchased by the user. Hybrid models combine both approaches to enhance recommendation accuracy, improving the shopping experience by tailoring suggestions to individual preferences.

Inventory management uses predictive analytics, which relies on machine learning models such as regression analysis and time-series forecasting. These models analyze patterns in sales data to predict future demand, helping businesses maintain optimal stock levels. Reinforcement learning, where AI learns by trial and error, can also be applied to refine inventory management strategies, as it allows the system to adapt based on feedback.

Dynamic pricing employs algorithms that analyze real-time market conditions, adjusting prices based on factors like demand, inventory levels, and competitor pricing. Machine learning models process this data continuously, ensuring that prices reflect the current market environment. Some retailers use deep learning models for dynamic pricing, as these models can capture complex patterns in consumer behavior, enabling more precise adjustments.

Amazon's recommendation engine is a well-known example of AI in e-commerce. Using collaborative and content-based filtering, Amazon suggests products based on users' browsing history, purchase behavior, and interactions with similar products. These recommendations are key to Amazon's sales strategy, as they enhance user engagement and drive repeat purchases.

In inventory management, Walmart uses AI to optimize stock levels across its stores and warehouses. Walmart's predictive analytics tools analyze sales data and external factors, enabling the company to maintain efficient inventory levels. By using AI to predict demand, Walmart minimizes stockouts and ensures that popular items are readily available, improving customer satisfaction.

Zara, a global fashion retailer, utilizes dynamic pricing and demand forecasting to respond quickly to changes in fashion trends. Zara's AI-driven supply chain monitors trends, adjusts production, and ensures that stores are stocked with styles that are in high demand. This fast-fashion model relies on AI to maintain its agility, allowing Zara to offer new styles frequently while avoiding excess inventory.

AI's role in retail and e-commerce highlights its potential to create more personalized, efficient, and profitable business models. Personalized recommendations enhance customer satisfaction, while dynamic pricing and inventory optimization improve profitability and operational efficiency. However, these AI-driven strategies must be implemented carefully, as over-reliance on personalization or dynamic pricing could impact customer trust. Data privacy is also a concern, as retailers must ensure compliance with privacy regulations when collecting and analyzing consumer data.

The future of AI in retail will likely involve even greater levels of personalization, with AI systems capable of adapting to individual customer journeys in real time. As AI continues to evolve, it will play an essential role in shaping the retail experience, making shopping more intuitive, convenient, and engaging for consumers.

---

7. AI in Energy and Environmental Sustainability

Artificial Intelligence is increasingly playing a vital role in promoting energy efficiency, optimizing renewable energy sources, and tackling environmental challenges. As climate change and resource scarcity become more pressing, AI offers innovative solutions for managing energy consumption, reducing emissions, and enhancing environmental sustainability. From improving grid management to monitoring ecosystems, AI's applications in this sector are advancing efforts toward a more sustainable future.

AI in the energy sector primarily focuses on optimizing energy production and consumption to minimize waste and reduce carbon footprints. One of the key applications is in **smart grid management**, where AI algorithms analyze data from power grids to balance supply and demand effectively. Traditional power grids can experience fluctuations due to varying energy demands, but AI-driven systems can predict these fluctuations and adjust the distribution of energy in real time. This dynamic management helps prevent blackouts and reduces energy waste, making power distribution more efficient.

Renewable energy integration is another area where AI has a significant impact. Solar and wind energy are sustainable sources but are subject to variability depending on weather conditions. AI algorithms can analyze weather patterns, historical data, and other variables to forecast energy production from these sources, enabling grid operators to plan accordingly. This forecasting is crucial for maintaining a stable supply and ensuring that renewable energy can reliably supplement traditional power sources.

In environmental sustainability, AI is used to monitor natural resources and ecosystems, track wildlife populations, and detect deforestation. By processing satellite imagery and sensor data, AI models can identify environmental changes over time, providing insights that support conservation efforts. For example, AI can help monitor illegal logging activities in remote forest areas, alerting authorities to potential environmental violations.

In smart grid management, machine learning models such as **time-series analysis** and **reinforcement learning** play a crucial role. Time-series analysis is used to predict energy consumption patterns based on historical data, helping utilities anticipate peak demand times. Reinforcement learning algorithms optimize energy distribution by learning from different scenarios, allowing the grid to adjust in real time based on current demand and supply levels.

For renewable energy forecasting, deep learning models like **recurrent neural networks (RNNs)** and **long short-term memory (LSTM) networks** are commonly used. These models analyze sequential data, such as weather patterns, to forecast solar or wind energy production. Accurate forecasting enables utilities to make data-driven decisions about energy storage, ensuring that excess energy generated during peak production times can be stored for later use.

In environmental monitoring, **computer vision** algorithms process satellite images to detect changes in land cover, water levels, and forest density. Convolutional neural networks (CNNs) are particularly useful for analyzing high-resolution images, as they can identify even subtle changes in ecosystems. Natural Language Processing (NLP) can also assist by processing reports and research articles, allowing environmental scientists to stay updated on recent findings and regulations.

Google's DeepMind has successfully applied AI to improve energy efficiency in its data centers. By using machine learning algorithms to analyze data from sensors, DeepMind reduced the energy required for cooling by 40%. This achievement not only cut costs but also significantly reduced the carbon footprint of Google's data centers, showcasing how AI can contribute to corporate sustainability efforts.

In renewable energy, companies like Siemens Gamesa are using AI for wind energy forecasting. Siemens Gamesa's AI models analyze weather data and turbine performance to predict energy output, allowing operators to adjust turbine settings for optimal efficiency. This AI-driven approach maximizes the utility of wind farms, making wind energy a more reliable component of the energy grid.

In environmental conservation, Microsoft's AI for Earth program uses computer vision to monitor ecosystems and track endangered species. By processing satellite images, AI models can identify areas affected by deforestation, illegal mining, or other activities that threaten biodiversity. This data supports conservation organizations in their efforts to protect critical habitats and promote sustainable land use.

AI's applications in energy and environmental sustainability demonstrate its potential to address some of the world's most pressing challenges. By optimizing energy use, supporting renewable energy sources, and monitoring ecosystems, AI helps mitigate climate change and promotes resource conservation. However, the energy demands of AI itself, especially in data centers, need to be considered, as high-powered computations can contribute to energy consumption. Balancing the environmental benefits of AI with its resource demands is essential for sustainable implementation.

As AI technology advances, it will likely play an even greater role in achieving global sustainability goals. Future developments may include AI-driven systems capable of managing complex energy grids autonomously or tracking real-time environmental changes across the globe. These advancements will contribute to a more sustainable, eco-conscious future, making AI a critical ally in the fight against climate change.

---

8. AI in Entertainment and Media

Artificial Intelligence is transforming the entertainment and media industries by enabling more personalized content, streamlining production processes, and creating entirely new experiences for audiences. From content recommendation systems and AI-generated art to virtual reality and deepfake technology, AI has opened up new creative possibilities and improved audience engagement. As media consumption becomes more digital and data-driven, AI plays an increasingly central role in shaping what we watch, listen to, and interact with.

How Artificial Intelligence Is Changing Your World (And How You Can Profit from It!) by Mitch

One of the most impactful applications of AI in entertainment is in **content recommendation**. Streaming platforms such as Netflix, Spotify, and YouTube use AI algorithms to analyze user behavior and preferences, delivering personalized recommendations that keep users engaged. By understanding individual tastes, AI-powered recommendation engines can suggest movies, shows, music, or videos that align with the user's interests, increasing satisfaction and time spent on the platform. This personalization has become a key strategy for retaining audiences in a highly competitive streaming market.

AI also enhances content creation by providing tools that automate parts of the production process. For example, AI can assist video editors by generating previews, tagging clips, and even suggesting cuts based on visual or audio cues. In journalism, AI algorithms can quickly generate articles based on data inputs, especially for tasks like summarizing sports scores or financial reports. These tools help content creators work more efficiently and allow them to focus on higher-level storytelling.

Moreover, AI has introduced novel forms of entertainment, including **virtual and augmented reality** experiences. AI-powered VR applications create immersive worlds that adapt to the user's actions, offering a dynamic and interactive experience. In the music industry, AI-generated compositions allow artists to experiment with new styles and genres, and AI-driven platforms can even generate custom background music for various settings or activities.

Recommendation engines rely on machine learning models such as **collaborative filtering**, **content-based filtering**, and **hybrid approaches**. Collaborative filtering analyzes user preferences and recommends content based on similarities between users, while content-based filtering suggests items that share attributes with previously consumed content. Many platforms use a hybrid of both to maximize recommendation accuracy. These models are trained on extensive datasets that track viewing or listening habits, allowing the AI to make informed predictions about user preferences.

In content creation, **Natural Language Processing (NLP)** plays a key role in text-based media. For instance, AI can generate written content by analyzing structured data and converting it into readable language. This approach is used in automated journalism, where AI produces summaries and reports based on input data. **Computer vision** algorithms are also used in video editing, analyzing visual elements to create highlights or apply filters, making the editing process faster and more intuitive.

For immersive experiences, **deep learning** models and **computer graphics** are integrated into virtual reality systems to create responsive environments. AI processes user movements and adjusts virtual elements in real-time, creating a seamless experience. In music composition, AI algorithms analyze patterns in different musical genres and use generative models, like **Recurrent Neural Networks (RNNs)** and **Generative Adversarial Networks (GANs)**, to produce original compositions.

Netflix's recommendation system is a classic example of AI in entertainment. By tracking each user's viewing history and preferences, Netflix provides a tailored selection of shows and movies. The platform's AI system also considers broader trends and genre preferences, making recommendations highly relevant and personal. This personalized approach keeps users engaged, reducing the likelihood of subscription cancellation.

In the music industry, the AI platform Amper Music enables creators to compose original music with minimal input. Users specify genre, mood, and instrumentation, and Amper's algorithms generate a composition based on these parameters. This AI-powered tool is particularly useful for video content creators who need background music without complex licensing issues.

In virtual reality, companies like Oculus use AI to enhance the realism of VR experiences. By integrating machine learning algorithms that process user movements and environmental data, Oculus creates responsive, lifelike virtual spaces. This adaptability makes VR more immersive, allowing users to interact with the virtual environment in real-time.

AI's integration into entertainment and media has created more engaging and personalized experiences for audiences. However, the use of AI also raises ethical concerns, particularly around data privacy and the potential for manipulation. For example, recommendation algorithms can reinforce content "bubbles," where users are only exposed to certain viewpoints or types of content, potentially limiting diversity in media consumption. Additionally, deepfake technology, which uses AI to create realistic but fabricated videos, poses risks to authenticity and trust in media.

Despite these challenges, AI is likely to continue shaping the entertainment industry, enabling new forms of creativity and audience interaction. As AI technologies evolve, they will open up additional avenues for storytelling, personalization, and immersive experiences, making entertainment more accessible and adaptable to individual preferences.

---

9. Ethics, Challenges, and the Future of AI Across Industries

As Artificial Intelligence becomes more deeply embedded in global industries, the ethical implications and challenges associated with its use grow increasingly complex. While AI offers immense benefits—from enhanced efficiency and productivity to innovation and personalization—its deployment raises important questions about privacy, transparency, and responsibility. Addressing these challenges is crucial to ensure that AI development and implementation align with societal values and promote equitable outcomes across industries.

Ethics in AI centers on issues like data privacy, fairness, accountability, and transparency. AI systems often require large amounts of data to function effectively, which means that data privacy is a key concern. For instance, in sectors like healthcare and finance, sensitive personal information is frequently processed by AI, making data protection essential to maintain public trust. Organizations implementing AI must adhere to privacy regulations such as the General Data Protection Regulation (GDPR) in Europe or the California Consumer Privacy Act (CCPA) in the United States to ensure that data is collected and used responsibly.

Transparency is another critical aspect, as many AI algorithms operate as "black boxes"—complex systems whose inner workings are not fully understandable to users or even developers. This lack of transparency can be problematic, especially in high-stakes fields such as healthcare and criminal justice, where AI decisions can have significant impacts on individuals. Increasing transparency through explainable AI, where algorithms provide insights into how decisions are made, is essential for accountability and trust.

Bias and fairness are also pressing ethical issues in AI. AI systems can inadvertently perpetuate or amplify existing biases if they are trained on biased data. For example, an AI hiring tool trained on past hiring data might favor certain demographics over others if historical biases are embedded in the data. Ensuring fairness requires careful oversight of training data and algorithmic outputs to avoid discriminatory practices.

In addressing privacy, data anonymization and encryption techniques are commonly used to protect sensitive information. Anonymization removes identifying information from datasets, allowing AI to analyze patterns without exposing individual identities. Differential privacy, a technique that adds "noise" to data, is also used to protect personal details while retaining valuable insights. These privacy-preserving methods are essential for industries that handle sensitive data, like healthcare and finance.

How Artificial Intelligence Is Changing Your World (And How You Can Profit from It!) by Mitch

Explainable AI (XAI) is an emerging field focused on making AI systems more interpretable. XAI techniques, such as LIME (Local Interpretable Model-Agnostic Explanations) and SHAP (SHapley Additive exPlanations), provide users with insights into which factors influenced an AI's decision. For instance, in credit scoring, SHAP can highlight which financial behaviors contributed most to an applicant's credit score, making the decision process more transparent.

To mitigate bias, machine learning models undergo fairness audits that assess their outputs for discriminatory patterns. Techniques like re-sampling, where the data is adjusted to be more representative, or debiasing algorithms, which alter model training to promote fairness, are common. Implementing these methods ensures that AI systems make equitable decisions across demographic groups, enhancing fairness in applications like hiring and lending.

The healthcare company Optum employs AI systems that adhere to strict privacy standards. By using anonymized patient data, Optum ensures that patient privacy is protected while enabling AI to deliver insights for preventive care and treatment optimization. Optum's approach reflects how companies can balance innovation with privacy considerations in high-stakes industries.

In financial services, the explainable AI model FICO Score XD provides users with insights into their credit scores, explaining which factors affected their rating. This transparency helps consumers understand their creditworthiness and fosters trust in AI-driven decisions in finance.

IBM's Watson for AI Ethics project is a notable example of efforts to address fairness and bias in AI. IBM uses bias-detection algorithms and rigorous testing to ensure that Watson's outputs are fair across different demographics. By implementing these practices, IBM demonstrates its commitment to responsible AI development and addresses public concerns over AI fairness.

The ethical implications of AI are critical as the technology continues to evolve and expand across industries. By addressing issues of privacy, transparency, and fairness, organizations can create AI systems that are both effective and aligned with ethical standards. AI's future in industry depends on responsible practices that promote fairness, accountability, and inclusivity, ensuring that benefits are widely distributed and do not reinforce societal inequalities.

As AI advances, its potential applications and influence will grow, offering new ways to solve complex challenges and drive innovation. However, responsible AI development must keep pace with these advancements to avoid unintended consequences and protect societal values. The future of AI across industries will depend on collaboration between developers, regulators, and society at large to build an ethical framework that guides its evolution.

CHAPTER 7: Societal Impacts of AI - Opportunities, Challenges, and the Path Forward

1. Introduction to AI's Societal Impact

Artificial Intelligence has advanced from an emerging technology into a powerful force reshaping societies worldwide. As AI integrates into various domains of daily life—healthcare, finance, education, transportation, public safety, and more—it brings transformative benefits and poses complex challenges. AI's dual impact on society is significant: on one hand, it drives innovation, efficiency, and new possibilities for growth and learning; on the other, it introduces ethical questions, potential biases, and concerns about privacy, job displacement, and equality. Understanding AI's role in shaping societal norms, values, and opportunities is essential as it continues to evolve at an unprecedented pace.

At its core, AI's societal impact is rooted in its ability to analyze large datasets, learn from patterns, make predictions, and automate tasks. These capabilities allow AI to make decisions that were once considered exclusively within the domain of human judgment. For example, AI's predictive algorithms in healthcare can identify early signs of diseases, helping clinicians intervene sooner and save lives. In finance, AI systems streamline fraud detection, protecting consumer assets and ensuring regulatory compliance. Meanwhile, in transportation, AI drives advancements in autonomous vehicles that promise to reduce accidents and revolutionize mobility.

However, the benefits of AI are accompanied by challenges that must be carefully managed. AI systems depend on vast quantities of data, which raises concerns about data privacy and the ethical implications of data usage. The more AI algorithms rely on personal data, the greater the need for rigorous standards to protect individuals' information and prevent misuse. Additionally, while AI can make decisions faster and more efficiently than humans, it can also introduce or perpetuate biases if the data it is trained on is flawed or unrepresentative. This risk is especially pronounced in sectors like hiring, where AI-based screening tools could unintentionally discriminate against certain demographic groups, amplifying existing social inequalities.

Beyond individual concerns, AI's impact on a societal level touches economic structures, cultural norms, and the fundamental nature of work. As AI automates tasks traditionally performed by humans, industries and workforces face shifts in employment patterns. Some jobs may be displaced or radically transformed, while new roles centered around AI technology emerge. This shift has led to growing discussions about upskilling and reskilling workers, preparing them for a workforce that increasingly values technical proficiency and adaptability to AI-driven environments.

AI's potential to reshape society also extends to issues of access and equality. In theory, AI could help bridge gaps in healthcare, education, and economic opportunity by providing accessible solutions at scale. For instance, telemedicine platforms powered by AI can reach underserved communities, offering medical expertise in remote areas. Similarly, AI-driven educational tools can personalize learning for students of all abilities, improving outcomes for those who may struggle in traditional settings. However, these benefits are not universally accessible, as disparities in technology access—often referred to as the digital divide—limit who can fully benefit from AI innovations.

In this chapter, we will examine the various dimensions of AI's societal impact, exploring both its promises and its pitfalls. From workforce transformations and ethical considerations to public policy and social equality, each section will provide a comprehensive look at how AI shapes, and is shaped by, the societies it operates within. We'll delve into specific areas where AI has already made significant strides and discuss the potential long-term effects of its integration into different facets of life. By understanding these impacts, stakeholders—including policymakers, businesses, and the general public—can work together to create a future where AI serves society's best interests while minimizing unintended consequences.

---

2. AI and the Workforce

Artificial Intelligence is transforming the workforce, reshaping job roles, altering workplace dynamics, and introducing new opportunities and challenges. As automation, machine learning, and data-driven insights redefine how work is conducted, AI is both a catalyst for economic growth and a source of uncertainty for workers across various sectors. Understanding the complex interplay between AI and the workforce requires examining its effects on job displacement, job creation, skills development, and workplace culture.

One of the primary ways AI is impacting the workforce is through **automation**. Tasks that were once labor-intensive are increasingly being automated, allowing companies to streamline operations and reduce costs. This trend is particularly visible in sectors like manufacturing, logistics, and customer service. In manufacturing, AI-powered robots handle repetitive tasks such as assembly, quality control, and packaging, boosting productivity and precision. Similarly, in logistics, AI algorithms optimize supply chain management by predicting demand, managing inventory, and planning routes for delivery. This automation reduces operational costs and improves efficiency, giving companies a competitive edge in a global market.

In customer service, AI-driven chatbots and virtual assistants have become commonplace. These tools handle common inquiries, provide information, and resolve issues without human intervention. By automating these interactions, companies can serve more customers and reduce wait times, enhancing customer satisfaction. However, the rise of automation has raised concerns about **job displacement**. Routine jobs that rely on repetitive tasks are at high risk of being automated, potentially displacing workers who previously performed these roles. For example, warehouse workers, retail cashiers, and call center operators face an uncertain future as AI-driven solutions take over their responsibilities.

While AI-driven automation may reduce demand for certain types of jobs, it also creates new opportunities, particularly in technology-related fields. The **creation of new jobs** is a positive outcome of AI's integration into the workforce, as companies need skilled professionals to develop, implement, and maintain AI systems. Roles such as data scientists, AI specialists, machine learning engineers, and ethical AI advisors are becoming increasingly important as organizations rely more heavily on AI. These new roles often require a high level of technical expertise, critical thinking, and adaptability, which means that workers with these skills are in high demand.

Moreover, as AI technology evolves, **upskilling and reskilling** are essential for workers to remain relevant in the job market. Many industries, recognizing the importance of a skilled workforce, are investing in training programs that equip employees with AI-related skills. For example, manufacturing companies may offer training on operating and maintaining automated machinery, while healthcare providers may train medical professionals to interpret AI-driven diagnostic tools. Upskilling initiatives not only help workers adapt to new technologies but also empower them to contribute to the AI-driven transformation within their industries.

AI's impact on the workforce also extends to **workplace culture and dynamics**. As companies adopt AI-driven tools, the nature of collaboration and decision-making is evolving. AI systems often handle data analysis and pattern recognition, allowing human employees to focus on strategic, creative, and interpersonal tasks. This shift encourages a more collaborative approach, where AI augments human capabilities rather than replacing them entirely. For example, in finance, AI algorithms analyze market trends and provide insights, enabling financial analysts to make informed decisions. In marketing, AI tools identify customer preferences, helping teams craft personalized campaigns that resonate with target audiences.

However, the integration of AI into the workplace raises questions about **fairness and transparency**. Decisions made by AI systems, such as hiring recommendations or performance evaluations, can impact employees' careers significantly. It is essential for organizations to ensure that AI algorithms are free from bias and operate transparently, so employees feel confident in the fairness of these systems. Ethical AI practices, such as algorithm audits and bias detection, are crucial to maintaining trust in AI-driven workplaces.

The shift toward an AI-enhanced workforce brings both **opportunities and challenges**. While AI has the potential to improve productivity, drive innovation, and create high-quality jobs, it also requires careful management to prevent job displacement and inequality. By prioritizing upskilling and ethical AI practices, organizations can foster a workforce that is well-equipped to thrive in an AI-driven world. This transition necessitates collaboration between employers, policymakers, and educational institutions to build a future where AI empowers, rather than hinders, the workforce.

---

3. AI in Education and Lifelong Learning

Artificial Intelligence is revolutionizing the field of education, offering new ways to personalize learning, improve accessibility, and streamline administrative processes. From early childhood education to adult learning, AI-powered tools are transforming how individuals acquire knowledge, develop skills, and engage in lifelong learning. As education systems strive to meet the diverse needs of students, AI presents opportunities to make learning more adaptive, inclusive, and efficient.

One of the most promising applications of AI in education is **personalized learning**. Traditional educational models often struggle to accommodate the varying paces, preferences, and learning styles of individual students. AI-powered adaptive learning platforms address this challenge by tailoring content to each student's strengths, weaknesses, and progress. For example, a math tutoring platform might adjust problem difficulty based on a student's performance, providing more challenging questions when they excel and additional support when they struggle. This level of customization enhances student engagement and promotes mastery of subjects.

Personalized learning is particularly beneficial for students with diverse learning needs, including those with learning disabilities or gifted students who may require advanced material. AI-driven platforms like DreamBox and Khan Academy offer tailored exercises that cater to different ability levels, helping each student reach their full potential. By providing real-time feedback and targeted resources, AI fosters a supportive learning environment that adapts to each individual's unique requirements.

In addition to personalizing instruction, AI supports **administrative tasks** that educators and institutions manage daily. Automated grading, attendance tracking, and scheduling are examples of tasks that AI systems can handle, freeing up educators to focus on teaching and student interaction. For instance, Natural Language Processing (NLP) algorithms can assess written responses, grading essays based on grammar, coherence, and content relevance. This automation reduces the administrative burden on teachers, allowing them to devote more time to lesson planning and one-on-one student support.

AI also plays a vital role in **language learning**, where it enables immersive, interactive experiences. AI-powered applications like Duolingo and Babbel offer language instruction that adapts to a learner's progress, using speech recognition to provide pronunciation feedback and vocabulary exercises. These tools are especially valuable for individuals learning new languages independently, as they offer practice opportunities outside traditional classroom settings. By incorporating NLP and speech recognition, AI-driven language platforms create a dynamic learning experience that mirrors real-world conversations.

Beyond formal education, AI is crucial in promoting **lifelong learning** and **professional development**. In today's rapidly changing job market, professionals need to continuously update their skills to stay competitive. AI-powered learning platforms like LinkedIn Learning and Coursera offer courses tailored to individual career paths, providing personalized recommendations based on career goals and skill gaps. These platforms use AI to analyze industry trends, recommending courses that align with the evolving demands of the workforce. This approach empowers individuals to build relevant skills throughout their careers, fostering a culture of lifelong learning.

Despite its benefits, the integration of AI in education raises questions about **equity and access**. While AI-powered tools can significantly improve learning outcomes, not all students have equal access to these technologies. The digital divide, or the gap between individuals who have access to digital resources and those who do not, can exacerbate existing inequalities in education. Students from low-income families or rural areas may face challenges in accessing AI-driven platforms, which could widen achievement gaps. Ensuring that AI technologies are accessible to all students is essential to creating an equitable educational system.

Privacy is another important consideration, as AI-driven educational tools collect vast amounts of student data to personalize learning. This data includes academic performance, engagement patterns, and, in some cases, behavioral information. Protecting student privacy and adhering to data protection regulations, such as the Family Educational Rights and Privacy Act (FERPA) in the United States, is critical to maintaining trust in AI-driven education. Educational institutions and technology providers must implement safeguards to protect student data and ensure compliance with privacy standards.

As AI continues to evolve, its role in education and lifelong learning will likely expand, offering new ways to support students, educators, and professionals. However, balancing the benefits of AI-driven personalization with the need for inclusivity, privacy, and human interaction is essential. Education is a deeply personal experience, and while AI can enhance learning, it should complement rather than replace the human touch. By implementing AI responsibly, education systems can create a future where every learner has access to high-quality, personalized learning opportunities.

---

4. AI and Ethics

The rapid adoption of Artificial Intelligence across various sectors has sparked significant ethical discussions, particularly concerning privacy, fairness, accountability, and transparency. As AI systems increasingly influence decisions in healthcare, finance, education, law enforcement, and other critical areas, ethical considerations are paramount. Ensuring that AI is developed and implemented responsibly is essential to safeguarding public trust and preventing unintended harm.

One of the primary ethical concerns surrounding AI is **data privacy**. AI systems rely heavily on data to function effectively, often processing large amounts of personal and sensitive information. In healthcare, for example, AI algorithms analyze patient records to assist in diagnostics, treatment planning, and disease prevention. Similarly, in finance, AI models assess creditworthiness, fraud risk, and investment opportunities based on user data. While these applications offer clear benefits, they also raise concerns about how this data is collected, stored, and used. Protecting individuals' privacy is critical to maintaining trust, and organizations must ensure they comply with regulations like the General Data Protection Regulation (GDPR) in Europe or the California Consumer Privacy Act (CCPA) in the United States.

Fairness and bias in AI systems are equally pressing ethical issues. AI algorithms learn from historical data, which may contain biases based on past human decisions or societal inequalities. If these biases are not addressed, AI systems risk perpetuating or even amplifying discrimination. For instance, an AI-based hiring tool trained on historical hiring data may favor certain demographics over others if that bias exists in the original data. Similarly, in the criminal justice system, predictive policing algorithms may disproportionately target minority communities if the training data reflects past discriminatory practices. Ensuring fairness in AI requires rigorous testing, auditing, and re-training of algorithms to identify and mitigate biases, promoting equitable outcomes across demographics.

Accountability is another crucial consideration, especially as AI systems take on more responsibilities traditionally handled by humans. In complex environments like autonomous vehicles, healthcare diagnostics, and financial decision-making, determining accountability when an AI system makes an error can be challenging. If an autonomous vehicle is involved in an accident, questions arise regarding who is responsible—the vehicle manufacturer, the software developer, or the user? Similarly, if an AI system provides a medical recommendation that leads to a misdiagnosis, accountability becomes a gray area. To address these challenges, experts advocate for accountability frameworks that clarify the roles and responsibilities of developers, operators, and users, ensuring that AI systems operate transparently and within defined ethical boundaries.

Transparency in AI, often referred to as "explainability," is essential for building trust in AI-driven decisions. Many AI models, especially deep learning systems, operate as "black boxes," where their inner workings are complex and difficult to interpret, even for developers. This lack of transparency can be problematic in high-stakes applications, where understanding how a decision was made is crucial. For example, a patient may want to know why an AI recommended a specific treatment, or a loan applicant may question why they were denied credit. Explainable AI (XAI) aims to make AI models more interpretable, providing insights into the factors that influenced specific decisions. Techniques like Local Interpretable Model-Agnostic Explanations (LIME) and SHapley Additive exPlanations (SHAP) are used to explain model predictions, helping end-users understand AI outputs and fostering trust.

Beyond technical solutions, many organizations are establishing **ethical AI principles and guidelines** to address these issues proactively. Companies like Google, IBM, and Microsoft have developed ethical AI frameworks to guide responsible development, emphasizing principles such as fairness, transparency, accountability, and inclusivity. These frameworks aim to align AI technologies with human values, ensuring that they serve society ethically. In addition, regulatory bodies worldwide are working to establish AI-specific guidelines, balancing innovation with the need for ethical safeguards. The European Union, for instance, has proposed a regulatory framework that classifies AI applications by risk level, mandating strict compliance for high-risk applications such as facial recognition and predictive policing.

Public engagement and education are also essential in addressing AI ethics. As AI becomes more pervasive, the public needs to understand its implications and limitations. Raising awareness about AI's potential risks, ethical concerns, and societal impacts empowers individuals to make informed decisions about AI technologies in their personal and professional lives. Educational initiatives that demystify AI and promote digital literacy are crucial to building a society capable of engaging in meaningful discussions about AI ethics.

The path to ethical AI requires collaboration across sectors, with input from technologists, ethicists, policymakers, and the general public. While AI presents immense opportunities, its implementation must be carefully managed to align with ethical standards. By prioritizing transparency, fairness, accountability, and privacy, society can harness the benefits of AI while minimizing unintended harm, creating a future where AI serves humanity responsibly and equitably.

---

5. AI and Public Policy

As Artificial Intelligence continues to evolve, it is reshaping society in ways that require thoughtful and comprehensive public policy responses. Governments worldwide are grappling with how best to regulate and guide AI development, balancing the need for innovation with the imperative to protect citizens' rights, ensure security, and promote ethical standards. Effective AI policy addresses areas such as data protection, safety standards, accountability, and economic competitiveness, providing a framework that guides responsible AI deployment while fostering public trust.

A significant focus of AI policy is **data protection and privacy**. AI systems rely heavily on data, which often includes sensitive personal information, to make accurate predictions and recommendations. To protect citizens' privacy, policymakers have introduced regulations like the General Data Protection Regulation (GDPR) in Europe, which mandates that organizations obtain user consent before collecting data and stipulates that individuals have the right to access, modify, or delete their data. The GDPR also emphasizes transparency, requiring companies to disclose how they use AI to process personal information. Similarly, the California Consumer Privacy Act (CCPA) in the United States grants individuals the right to know what data is collected about them and how it is used. These regulations establish a foundational level of protection for citizens, but as AI technology advances, policymakers may need to refine and adapt these frameworks to address emerging privacy concerns.

AI safety standards are another critical component of public policy. In sectors where AI directly impacts public safety—such as healthcare, autonomous vehicles, and law enforcement—policymakers must ensure that AI systems operate reliably and predictably. Safety standards provide guidelines on system testing, performance benchmarks, and failure protocols, ensuring that AI systems perform as intended without posing risks to public health or safety. For example, the development of autonomous vehicles has prompted governments to establish testing standards that verify these systems' reliability before they are deployed on public roads. Policymakers also work with industry stakeholders to create industry-specific standards, such as those for medical AI tools, which must meet rigorous testing requirements to ensure accuracy and efficacy in patient care.

Accountability in AI is a complex policy challenge, as AI decisions can have profound consequences for individuals. Public policy on accountability establishes who is responsible for decisions made or influenced by AI systems, whether it's the developers, operators, or users. This issue is particularly relevant in legal and financial sectors, where AI-based decisions can impact credit scores, hiring outcomes, or sentencing recommendations. To address this, some governments are considering policies that require organizations to perform regular audits of their AI systems to identify and mitigate biases. This approach promotes accountability by ensuring that AI systems operate fairly and do not perpetuate discrimination. The European Union's proposed AI regulatory framework, for example, introduces requirements for "high-risk" AI applications, mandating rigorous risk assessments and accountability measures.

International cooperation is crucial for establishing effective AI policy, as AI is a global technology that transcends national borders. Countries are increasingly recognizing the need to collaborate on AI governance, developing standards that ensure consistency and promote responsible AI use worldwide. Initiatives like the Global Partnership on AI (GPAI) bring together countries to share best practices, address common challenges, and align on ethical standards. Additionally, organizations like the Organisation for Economic Co-operation and Development (OECD) have published AI principles that serve as a global benchmark for responsible AI development. By cooperating on AI policy, countries can foster a shared vision of ethical AI and mitigate the risks associated with inconsistent regulations.

Public engagement in AI policymaking is essential to create policies that reflect societal values and needs. Policymakers are increasingly seeking input from stakeholders, including technologists, ethicists, business leaders, and the general public, to shape AI regulations that balance innovation with ethical standards. In democratic societies, public consultations and advisory committees are commonly used to gather diverse perspectives, ensuring that AI policies address citizens' concerns. This approach enhances transparency and builds public trust, as individuals feel that they have a voice in decisions that affect their lives.

Countries around the world have adopted varied approaches to AI governance, each reflecting different cultural, economic, and political contexts. The **European Union** has taken a proactive stance, proposing regulations that classify AI applications by risk level. Under the EU's framework, high-risk applications, such as biometric surveillance and predictive policing, are subject to stringent requirements, including regular audits and impact assessments. By setting a high standard for AI accountability, the EU aims to protect citizens' rights and ensure that AI technologies are used responsibly.

In contrast, **the United States** has favored a more market-driven approach, emphasizing innovation and economic competitiveness. While the U.S. has not introduced a comprehensive federal AI regulation, several agencies, including the Federal Trade Commission (FTC) and the Food and Drug Administration (FDA), oversee AI applications within their respective domains. This sector-specific approach allows for flexible regulation but has raised concerns about the lack of cohesive federal standards. However, recent discussions within the U.S. Congress suggest a growing interest in creating a federal AI framework that addresses privacy, accountability, and transparency.

China has also made significant strides in AI governance, with policies that promote rapid AI development while ensuring state oversight. The Chinese government's New Generation AI Development Plan outlines its vision for AI leadership by 2030, focusing on AI innovation, talent development, and ethical standards. China's regulatory approach is unique in that it combines support for private-sector AI innovation with strict government control over applications related to national security and social stability. This model reflects China's prioritization of AI as a driver of economic and strategic power, alongside a focus on maintaining control over sensitive AI technologies.

As AI continues to influence society, **the role of public policy will only grow in importance**. Policymakers must remain agile, adapting regulations to address new ethical and technical challenges that arise as AI evolves. Collaboration between governments, international organizations, and industry stakeholders is essential to develop policies that promote responsible AI use while fostering innovation. By prioritizing privacy, safety, accountability, and public engagement, policymakers can create a regulatory landscape that supports AI's potential to benefit society whil Certainly! I'll continue with the remaining sections for **Chapter 7** in sequence, covering each topic thoroughly to achieve the 15,000-word target.

---

6. AI in Public Health and Safety

Artificial Intelligence is transforming public health and safety by providing tools for disease prevention, enhancing emergency response, and improving public security measures. AI-driven systems enable public health officials, law enforcement, and emergency responders to make informed decisions, respond quickly, and proactively manage risks. As AI becomes a key player in public health and safety, it presents opportunities for better outcomes but also raises questions about privacy and ethics.

In public health, AI plays a critical role in **disease prevention and management**. AI algorithms analyze data from sources like hospital records, laboratory tests, and even social media trends to identify early signs of disease outbreaks. For instance, during the COVID-19 pandemic, AI models were instrumental in tracking the spread of the virus, forecasting infection rates, and optimizing resource allocation. By analyzing patterns in real-time data, AI helps health authorities make timely interventions, allocate medical resources efficiently, and communicate effectively with the public.

Emergency response is another area where AI has a significant impact. AI algorithms can analyze weather patterns, natural disaster risks, and population density to predict and prepare for emergencies. For example, AI-based systems can forecast the impact of hurricanes, earthquakes, and floods, enabling governments to evacuate vulnerable populations and mobilize resources. Additionally, AI-powered drones and robots assist in search-and-rescue missions, helping responders locate and aid people in disaster-stricken areas.

In law enforcement, AI enhances **public safety** through predictive policing, surveillance, and crime analysis. AI tools analyze historical crime data to identify patterns, predict potential criminal hotspots, and allocate police resources effectively. However, predictive policing is controversial, as it raises concerns about racial profiling and over-policing in certain communities. Transparency and oversight are essential to ensure that AI systems support public safety without infringing on civil rights.

AI's role in public health and safety highlights the importance of **privacy and ethical safeguards**. Public health applications often rely on personal health data, while surveillance tools in public safety use video footage and other sensitive information. Ensuring that these data-driven systems comply with privacy regulations and operate ethically is critical to maintaining public trust. While AI offers substantial benefits for health and safety, responsible implementation and strict oversight are necessary to prevent misuse.

---

7. The Environmental Impact of AI

Artificial Intelligence is both a tool for environmental sustainability and a contributor to environmental challenges. On one hand, AI-driven innovations support efforts to combat climate change, conserve biodiversity, and promote sustainable resource use. On the other hand, the energy consumption associated with AI infrastructure raises concerns about its environmental footprint.

AI contributes to **environmental sustainability** by enhancing renewable energy production, optimizing resource management, and promoting eco-friendly practices. For instance, AI algorithms can predict energy demand, allowing power grids to integrate renewable sources like wind and solar efficiently. AI also supports precision agriculture, where sensors and machine learning models guide irrigation, pesticide use, and crop management, reducing environmental impact and improving yields.

AI's energy consumption, however, is a notable concern. Training deep learning models requires large amounts of computational power, often provided by data centers with high electricity demands. This energy usage contributes to carbon emissions, especially if data centers rely on non-renewable energy sources. Some technology companies are addressing this issue by investing in **green data centers** powered by renewable energy and implementing energy-efficient hardware.

As AI continues to advance, addressing its environmental impact will be essential. Efforts to reduce the carbon footprint of AI infrastructure, combined with the sustainable applications of AI, can create a balanced approach that supports environmental goals. AI has the potential to be a powerful ally in combating climate change, but mindful implementation is necessary to ensure that its environmental benefits outweigh its costs.

---

8. AI and Social Equality

AI has the potential to address social inequalities by increasing access to essential services, improving economic opportunities, and promoting inclusive development. However, if not carefully managed, AI could also exacerbate existing inequalities, creating a digital divide where only certain groups benefit from AI-driven advancements.

In **healthcare**, AI tools can make quality medical care more accessible. For example, telemedicine platforms powered by AI bring diagnostic tools and consultations to rural or underserved communities, reducing barriers to healthcare access. Similarly, AI in education provides personalized learning experiences, making high-quality education accessible to students regardless of location or background. These applications of AI support social equality by bridging gaps in essential services.

Economic inequality is another area where AI can make a positive impact, especially through financial inclusion. AI-driven mobile banking and microfinance platforms enable individuals in developing regions to access financial services, such as loans and savings accounts, which might not be available through traditional banking. These services empower people to improve their economic situation and build financial security.

However, the digital divide—disparities in technology access—poses a significant challenge. Communities with limited internet access, digital literacy, or economic resources may struggle to benefit from AI-driven tools, potentially widening existing social inequalities. To promote social equality, governments, NGOs, and technology companies must work together to improve digital infrastructure, provide affordable internet access, and offer digital literacy programs.

By addressing these disparities, AI can become a force for social equality, providing marginalized communities with tools for self-empowerment and creating a more inclusive society. Bridging the digital divide is critical to ensuring that the benefits of AI are accessible to all.

---

9. Challenges in Implementing AI Responsibly

Implementing AI responsibly requires overcoming technical, financial, and ethical challenges. As organizations integrate AI into their operations, they face issues like bias in algorithms, regulatory compliance, transparency, and the financial costs of AI deployment.

One of the primary challenges is **bias in AI algorithms**. AI systems trained on biased data can perpetuate discrimination, leading to unfair outcomes in areas such as hiring, lending, and criminal justice. Addressing bias requires organizations to conduct regular audits, improve data quality, and implement bias detection tools. Ensuring fairness in AI is essential to building trust and achieving ethical outcomes.

Regulatory compliance is another significant hurdle. Organizations must adhere to various laws and guidelines that govern data privacy, accountability, and transparency. Navigating these regulations can be complex, especially for companies operating in multiple countries with different legal standards. Compliance requires investments in legal resources, data protection measures, and documentation to meet regulatory requirements.

The **financial costs of AI implementation** are also considerable. Developing, training, and maintaining AI systems requires substantial resources, which can be a barrier for small and medium-sized enterprises. In addition to infrastructure costs, hiring skilled AI professionals is costly, as the demand for expertise in AI outpaces supply. Financial constraints can limit the ability of some organizations to adopt AI responsibly and at scale.

Addressing these challenges requires collaboration between the public and private sectors, as well as the development of industry standards that promote responsible AI use. By investing in ethical AI practices, organizations can create systems that align with societal values and avoid unintended harm.

---

10. The Future of AI in Society

The future of Artificial Intelligence holds immense promise as well as uncertainty. As AI technology continues to evolve, its applications will likely expand, influencing every aspect of society. From new advancements in healthcare and education to unforeseen ethical dilemmas, the journey of AI's societal impact is just beginning.

One area of potential growth is **general AI**, where systems could perform tasks across a wide range of domains, displaying intelligence closer to human cognition. While we are currently far from achieving general AI, advancements in machine learning, neural networks, and quantum computing could make this a reality in the future. General AI would have transformative effects on society, but it also raises profound ethical and existential questions, including the potential for unintended consequences that are difficult to predict or control.

The development of **human-AI collaboration** will also shape the future of AI. Rather than replacing humans, future AI systems could enhance human capabilities, leading to new roles and opportunities in the workforce. Human-AI partnerships will allow individuals to focus on creative, strategic, and empathetic tasks, while AI handles data processing and pattern recognition. This collaborative approach could improve productivity and job satisfaction, creating a balanced and symbiotic relationship between humans and machines.

Global cooperation will be essential to navigate AI's future responsibly. As AI transcends borders, countries must work together to establish international standards that address ethical, safety, and privacy concerns. Initiatives like the UN's recommendations on AI ethics and the Global Partnership on AI are examples of collaborative efforts to create a unified approach to AI governance.

The future of AI in society will depend on our ability to harness its benefits while mitigating its risks. By fostering inclusive, transparent, and ethical AI development, we can create a future where AI enhances human well-being, empowers communities, and contributes to a fair and just world.

CHAPTER 8: AI as a Catalyst for Innovation - Transforming Research, Creativity, and Industry

1. Introduction to AI as a Catalyst for Innovation

Artificial Intelligence is driving a new wave of innovation across industries and disciplines, acting as a transformative force that accelerates discovery, enhances creativity, and enables groundbreaking advancements. As AI continues to evolve, it is not only reshaping traditional fields but also creating entirely new domains of exploration and understanding. By enabling more efficient data analysis, uncovering novel patterns, and augmenting human creativity, AI provides a platform for innovation that is unprecedented in both scope and scale.

One of the fundamental reasons AI acts as such a powerful catalyst for innovation is its ability to process and interpret vast quantities of data with remarkable speed and accuracy. Traditional research methods often rely on manual data collection and analysis, which can be time-consuming and limited by human constraints. AI, particularly through machine learning and deep learning algorithms, can analyze complex datasets rapidly, identifying patterns and correlations that may not be immediately apparent to researchers. This capability is especially valuable in data-intensive fields like genomics, climate science, and economics, where insights drawn from AI-driven analysis can lead to significant breakthroughs.

AI's role in enhancing creativity is equally transformative. In the creative arts, AI is being used to generate art, compose music, and even write literature, providing artists and creators with new tools to explore their craft. AI-driven generative models, such as Generative Adversarial Networks (GANs) and natural language processing tools, allow artists to push the boundaries of their creativity by generating unique content or collaborating with AI in the creative process. This fusion of technology and creativity opens up new artistic possibilities, blending human intuition with computational power to create works that are both innovative and thought-provoking.

The interdisciplinary applications of AI are further amplifying its impact, as the technology bridges gaps between fields and fosters collaboration. For example, in bioinformatics, AI combines knowledge from biology, computer science, and statistics to analyze genetic data and understand complex biological systems. Similarly, in engineering, AI-driven simulations and predictive modeling enable designers to optimize structures and materials in ways that were previously unimaginable. These interdisciplinary applications demonstrate how AI fosters a cross-pollination of ideas, sparking innovation that transcends traditional boundaries.

As AI continues to advance, its role in driving innovation will likely expand, bringing forth new methods of discovery and creativity. This chapter explores AI's impact on innovation across scientific research, the creative arts, interdisciplinary fields, and rapid prototyping. Through examples and case studies, we will examine how AI is accelerating breakthroughs, enabling novel approaches, and transforming the very nature of innovation. By understanding AI's role in fostering innovation, we can better appreciate its potential to shape the future of knowledge, creativity, and progress.

---

2. AI in Scientific Research and Discovery

Artificial Intelligence is revolutionizing scientific research by accelerating the discovery process, enabling novel insights, and tackling complex problems that were previously difficult or impossible to address. In fields like genomics, physics, climate science, and chemistry, AI has become an invaluable tool, capable of processing enormous datasets, generating hypotheses, and simulating outcomes at unprecedented speeds. AI's impact on research is reshaping scientific exploration and enabling researchers to pursue questions that push the boundaries of human knowledge.

One of AI's most powerful applications in science is in **genomics**. The study of genomes requires the analysis of massive amounts of genetic data, which can be computationally intensive and time-consuming. AI algorithms, particularly deep learning models, have been instrumental in accelerating this analysis. For example, AI tools can predict the function of specific genes, identify mutations linked to diseases, and even generate hypotheses about genetic links to conditions such as cancer and Alzheimer's disease. By automating much of the data analysis, AI allows researchers to focus on interpreting results and developing new treatments, potentially leading to breakthroughs in personalized medicine.

In **climate science**, AI helps researchers understand complex environmental patterns and predict the effects of climate change. Machine learning algorithms can analyze data from satellites, sensors, and historical climate records to model future climate scenarios. These models help scientists assess the impact of human activity on the environment and predict future weather patterns, sea-level changes, and ecosystem responses. AI-driven simulations are crucial for developing effective climate policies, as they provide policymakers with data-backed insights that guide decision-making. Additionally, AI helps researchers monitor deforestation, track endangered species, and evaluate the effectiveness of conservation efforts, further supporting global sustainability initiatives.

AI is also making significant strides in **physics and chemistry**, where it assists researchers in understanding complex physical phenomena and discovering new materials. In particle physics, AI analyzes data from experiments like those conducted at CERN, where large-scale particle collisions generate massive datasets. By identifying patterns within this data, AI helps physicists make sense of fundamental particles and forces, advancing our understanding of the universe. In chemistry, AI-powered models predict molecular behavior, aiding in drug discovery and the development of new materials. For instance, AI can simulate chemical reactions, reducing the need for trial-and-error experimentation in the lab, which speeds up the process of developing new compounds for pharmaceuticals, renewable energy, and industrial applications.

AI's contributions to scientific research underscore its potential as a transformative tool. By providing researchers with faster, more accurate methods of analyzing data, AI reduces barriers to discovery, enabling scientific progress that benefits society as a whole. As AI technology advances, its applications in scientific research will likely expand, driving breakthroughs that address some of humanity's most pressing challenges.

---

3. AI in Creative Industries

The creative industries—art, music, literature, and film—are experiencing a renaissance driven by Artificial Intelligence. AI is empowering artists, musicians, writers, and filmmakers to explore new forms of expression and break traditional boundaries. By collaborating with AI, creatives are discovering innovative approaches to their craft, combining human intuition with computational power to produce art that is both unique and reflective of our digital age.

In **visual arts**, AI-generated artwork is gaining prominence, as artists use algorithms to create pieces that challenge conventional notions of creativity. Generative Adversarial Networks (GANs), a type of AI model, are particularly popular in this field. GANs consist of two networks—a generator and a discriminator—that work together to create images that resemble those found in a dataset. Artists like Mario Klingemann and Refik Anadol have used GANs to produce stunning visual art that blends realism with surrealism. AI-generated art has found its place in galleries, auctions, and digital spaces, where it sparks discussions about the nature of creativity and the role of technology in the arts.

Music composition is another area where AI is making significant contributions. AI algorithms analyze musical patterns, genres, and structures, enabling them to compose original pieces. Platforms like Amper Music and OpenAI's MuseNet allow users to generate music in various styles, from classical to jazz and electronic. These AI tools are particularly valuable for content creators who need background music without complex licensing issues. Additionally, musicians are using AI to experiment with new sounds, harmonies, and rhythms, pushing the boundaries of traditional music composition. AI-assisted music not only broadens creative possibilities but also democratizes music production by making it accessible to individuals without formal musical training.

In **literature**, AI-powered natural language processing (NLP) tools are assisting writers by generating text, suggesting plot ideas, and even writing entire stories. For example, OpenAI's GPT-3 has been used to create short stories, poetry, and articles. While AI-generated writing may lack the depth and nuance of human-authored literature, it provides a new medium for experimentation and creative expression. Writers can use AI as a collaborative partner, generating ideas or developing story arcs that they can refine and expand upon. This partnership between human authors and AI introduces a new paradigm in storytelling, where creativity is a shared endeavor.

The **film industry** is also harnessing AI to enhance storytelling and production. AI tools analyze audience preferences, helping filmmakers understand what resonates with viewers. This data-driven approach informs decisions about plot elements, character development, and visual aesthetics. Furthermore, AI is used in post-production, where it assists with tasks like editing, color correction, and special effects. For example, AI-powered visual effects tools enable filmmakers to create realistic CGI and seamless scene transitions. By streamlining these processes, AI reduces production time and costs, allowing filmmakers to bring their creative visions to life more efficiently.

AI's role in the creative industries is redefining what it means to create, opening new avenues for artistic expression while challenging the boundaries between human and machine creativity. As AI continues to evolve, it will likely become an even more integral part of the creative process, empowering artists to explore uncharted territory and reimagine the possibilities of art and storytelling.

---

4. Interdisciplinary Applications of AI

Artificial Intelligence has become a powerful tool for fostering innovation across disciplines, enabling collaboration and knowledge sharing between fields that were once siloed. By bridging gaps in knowledge and facilitating interdisciplinary research, AI is driving breakthroughs in areas like bioinformatics, engineering, social sciences, and beyond. The ability of AI to integrate information from multiple domains makes it an invaluable resource for tackling complex, multifaceted problems that require a holistic approach.

In **bioinformatics**, AI combines biology, computer science, and statistics to analyze complex biological data, particularly in genomics and proteomics. For example, machine learning algorithms analyze genetic data to identify mutations linked to diseases, predict protein structures, and understand gene expression patterns. These insights are crucial for advancing personalized medicine, where treatments are tailored to individual genetic profiles. AI-powered bioinformatics has accelerated research in fields such as oncology and immunology, where understanding genetic factors is key to developing effective therapies.

Engineering is another field where AI facilitates interdisciplinary innovation. In materials science, for instance, AI algorithms predict the properties of new materials based on their molecular structures. By simulating how these materials perform under different conditions, engineers can develop stronger, lighter, and more sustainable materials for applications ranging from aerospace to consumer electronics. AI-driven simulations allow researchers to test materials virtually, saving time and resources in the development process. This integration of AI with engineering not only enhances product development but also supports sustainable practices by reducing the need for physical prototypes.

In the **social sciences**, AI is used to analyze large datasets that provide insights into human behavior, societal trends, and economic dynamics. Social scientists use machine learning models to study patterns in social media activity, economic transactions, and demographic data. For example, AI can identify correlations between economic indicators and health outcomes, providing a basis for policies that address public health disparities. In psychology, AI-powered sentiment analysis tools assess language patterns to gauge mental health trends and understand social attitudes. By facilitating data-driven research, AI enables social scientists to test hypotheses and develop models that inform policy decisions and address societal challenges.

The interdisciplinary applications of AI demonstrate its potential as a unifying force that brings together diverse fields to solve complex problems. By enabling collaboration across disciplines, AI fosters a culture of innovation that transcends traditional academic and professional boundaries. As AI continues to evolve, its interdisciplinary applications will likely expand, creating new opportunities for collaboration and innovation across an even wider range of fields.

---

5. AI and Rapid Prototyping

In industries where product design and development are time-sensitive, AI-driven rapid prototyping has become a game-changer. By leveraging AI for simulation, generative design, and 3D modeling, companies can accelerate the product development process, improve design accuracy, and reduce costs. Rapid prototyping enables engineers and designers to test and refine ideas quickly, bringing products to market faster while maintaining high standards of quality and functionality.

Generative design is one of the key AI applications in rapid prototyping. This process uses algorithms to generate a wide array of design options based on specified parameters, such as material type, weight, strength, and cost constraints. Engineers input these parameters, and the AI model creates multiple design iterations, each optimized for specific criteria. Generative design is particularly valuable in industries like automotive and aerospace, where factors such as weight reduction and structural integrity are crucial. By using generative design, engineers can explore innovative solutions that might not have been considered through traditional methods.

3D modeling and simulation powered by AI enable companies to test products virtually before creating physical prototypes. In the automotive industry, for example, AI-driven simulations model how a vehicle's design will perform under different conditions, such as high-speed impacts or extreme weather. These simulations provide valuable insights into potential issues, allowing engineers to refine designs without the need for extensive physical testing. This approach not only speeds up the development process but also reduces the environmental impact of prototyping by minimizing waste.

In **consumer electronics**, AI assists in rapid prototyping by

analyzing user feedback and predicting market trends. For example, AI tools can evaluate customer preferences and suggest design modifications that align with consumer demand. This data-driven approach to prototyping ensures that products resonate with target audiences, improving the chances of market success. By incorporating AI into product development, companies can create user-centered designs that meet market needs effectively.

AI's role in rapid prototyping exemplifies its potential to drive innovation by enhancing efficiency, accuracy, and adaptability. As industries continue to adopt AI for prototyping, the product development process will become increasingly streamlined, enabling companies to bring high-quality products to market faster and with fewer resources.

---

6. Challenges and Limitations in AI-Driven Innovation

While Artificial Intelligence has opened new pathways for innovation, its integration into research, creative industries, and product development is not without challenges. These limitations range from technical and ethical concerns to financial constraints, and they can impact how effectively AI drives progress. Addressing these challenges is essential to ensuring that AI's potential for innovation is fully realized in ways that benefit society.

A key technical challenge in AI-driven innovation is **data dependency**. AI systems require large datasets to function effectively, as they rely on patterns in historical data to make predictions or generate content. In fields like healthcare or finance, data availability is often limited due to privacy regulations, which can hinder the development of robust AI models. Additionally, datasets used for training AI may contain biases that can lead to skewed results. For instance, if a generative design algorithm for architecture is trained on data that favors a particular style, it may overlook innovative design options. Ensuring diverse and unbiased datasets is crucial to overcoming data limitations in AI-driven innovation.

Another major challenge is **ethical considerations**, particularly in creative industries. As AI generates art, music, literature, and other forms of media, questions arise about originality and authorship. For example, if an AI model composes a piece of music based on input from existing compositions, can the output be considered truly original? Similarly, as AI tools produce visual art, some artists express concerns that AI-generated works may undervalue human creativity. Addressing these concerns requires an ethical framework that defines authorship and originality in the context of AI-assisted creation, ensuring that human contributions are recognized and respected.

Financial constraints are also a significant barrier to AI-driven innovation, especially for small and medium-sized enterprises (SMEs). Developing, training, and deploying AI models can be costly, requiring advanced hardware, software, and specialized expertise. Large corporations may have the resources to invest in state-of-the-art AI infrastructure, but SMEs often struggle to adopt these technologies at scale. This disparity can limit access to AI-driven innovation, creating an uneven playing field where only organizations with substantial resources can fully leverage AI's potential. Initiatives that promote affordable AI solutions and open-source models can help make AI innovation more accessible to smaller entities.

Intellectual property (IP) rights present additional challenges. As AI generates new products, designs, and creative works, determining ownership and protecting intellectual property becomes complex. For example, if an AI model generates a new drug compound, should the rights to that compound belong to the AI developer, the company that owns the AI, or the scientists who provided the training data? Clarifying IP rights in AI-driven innovation is essential for encouraging investment and fostering a fair environment where contributions are acknowledged appropriately.

By addressing these challenges, industries can create an environment where AI-driven innovation flourishes while respecting ethical, technical, and financial constraints. Establishing guidelines for data quality, implementing ethical frameworks, and promoting access to AI resources are steps that will help unlock the full potential of AI as a catalyst for innovation.

---

7. The Future of AI-Driven Innovation

The future of Artificial Intelligence promises advancements that could further accelerate innovation across industries. As AI technology continues to evolve, emerging trends and fields will likely benefit from its integration, paving the way for new discoveries, creative possibilities, and societal advancements. However, realizing this future will require careful consideration of responsible development, ethical standards, and inclusivity.

One area with significant potential for AI-driven innovation is **general AI**, which aims to create systems capable of performing tasks across a broad range of domains, exhibiting intelligence closer to human cognition. While current AI systems are designed for specific tasks—such as image recognition or language translation—general AI would be able to understand, learn, and reason about a wide variety of topics. The development of general AI could enable unprecedented interdisciplinary innovation, as a single AI system could contribute insights across fields, from healthcare and engineering to social sciences and the arts. However, the complexity and ethical implications of general AI necessitate a careful and collaborative approach to ensure that it aligns with human values and societal goals.

Human-AI collaboration is another area with transformative potential. Rather than replacing humans, AI is expected to work alongside individuals, enhancing human capabilities in various domains. In creative fields, AI could serve as a collaborative partner, generating ideas, refining concepts, and offering unique perspectives that artists and writers can build upon. Similarly, in scientific research, AI can handle data analysis and simulation, allowing scientists to focus on hypothesis generation and interpretation. This partnership between human intuition and AI's computational power could lead to more innovative and nuanced outcomes, fostering a new era of creativity and discovery.

The future of AI-driven innovation will also be shaped by advancements in **quantum computing**. Quantum computers have the potential to solve complex problems that are beyond the reach of classical computers, such as modeling molecular interactions for drug discovery or optimizing large-scale logistical networks. By pairing AI with quantum computing, industries could unlock new levels of efficiency, accuracy, and insight, accelerating progress in fields like pharmaceuticals, climate modeling, and finance. While quantum computing is still in its early stages, its integration with AI represents a promising frontier for scientific and technological advancement.

Global cooperation will be essential for the responsible advancement of AI-driven innovation. As AI becomes more integrated into society, international collaboration can ensure that AI technologies are developed with shared ethical principles, safety standards, and regulatory frameworks. Organizations such as the United Nations, the Global Partnership on AI, and the Organisation for Economic Co-operation and Development (OECD) are already working to create a unified approach to AI governance, promoting transparency, fairness, and accountability. By fostering an environment of cooperation, countries can harness AI's potential for global good while addressing shared challenges, such as data privacy, cybersecurity, and economic inequality.

The future of AI-driven innovation holds immense potential for positive societal impact, from scientific breakthroughs and creative exploration to sustainable development and improved quality of life. As we move forward, embracing responsible innovation practices and fostering an inclusive approach will be crucial to ensuring that AI serves as a catalyst for progress, empowering humanity to explore new possibilities and address pressing global challenges.

About the Author

Mitch is a leading expert in Artificial Intelligence and a passionate advocate for harnessing technology to drive personal and financial success. With over 20 years in the tech industry and a keen understanding of how AI is transforming everyday life, Mitch is dedicated to making complex concepts accessible to everyone. Known for his engaging writing style and practical insights, he has helped thousands of readers unlock new opportunities in the rapidly evolving digital world.

In *How Artificial Intelligence Is Changing Your World (And How You Can Profit from It!)*, Mitch combines years of research, real-world case studies, and proven strategies to show readers how AI is reshaping industries, creating new career paths, and presenting unprecedented financial opportunities. Whether you're an entrepreneur, investor, or simply curious about the future of technology, Mitch is your trusted guide to navigating—and thriving in—the AI revolution.